How To Build
Network Marketing

VOLUME ONE

Step-By-Step
Creation of MLM
Professionals

TOM "BIG AL" SCHREITER

For information, contact:

Fortune Network Publishing
PO Box 890084
Houston, TX 77289 USA
Telephone: +1 (281) 280-9800

ISBN: 1-892366-21-5
ISBN-13: 978-1-892366-21-4

DEDICATION

This book is dedicated to network marketers everywhere.

I travel the world 240+ days each year. Let me know if you want me to stop in your area and conduct a live Big Al training.

http://www.BigAlSeminars.com

Get 7 mini-reports of amazing, easy sentences that create new, hot prospects.

Sign up today at:
http://www.BigAlReport.com

Other great Big Al Books available at:

http://www.BigAlBooks.com

Table of Contents

PREFACE

This is just a start - not everything.

Leadership is a huge topic and skill. This book certainly won't begin to cover all the principles and skills we need to master. When writing this book, I had to decide where to start, and where to stop. No one wants to read 1,000 pages of leadership philosophy. No one wants to memorize 100 different leadership principles. No one wants to simultaneously master 200 different leadership skills. And what about the "how to" methods to implement all those things?

So if you are looking for one book to do it all, this isn't the book. This book is only a start. But, we have to start somewhere, right? If we don't know what we don't know, starting is the best first option. So let's get started with learning a few things about leadership now.

This book will have some philosophy, some principles, some skills, some "how to" methods, but it certainly won't have them all. As in anything, we learn some things first, and then later we learn more. That is why this book is called, "Volume One."

"How to Build Network Marketing Leaders Volume One: Step-By-Step Creation of MLM Professionals" addresses the 600-pound gorilla in the room: problems.

-- Tom "Big Al" Schreiter

"I am lazy. Just give me the secret."

If you can only read this far into this book, the secret is easy.

Implementing the secret will require that we learn some new skills. Ah, that's a little harder. Yes, there is always a "catch."

Try this little routine:

Step 1: Think of all the books, audios, and seminars about how to be successful in network marketing.

Step 2: Now think about all the manuals and training programs produced by network marketing companies.

Step 3: Now, put all this wisdom into one large pile.

Result?

You now have a very big pile of stuff that few people would ever read.

Wouldn't it be nice to reduce all of this network marketing success wisdom to **one simple phrase**?

Well, here's the secret. The one simple phrase that sums up all you need to know to become a superstar in network marketing. Ready? Here it is.

To be successful in network marketing, all you have to do is:

Build leaders and make them successful!

That's it. That's the total essence of that enormous pile of wisdom.

Leaders make your life easy. Leaders make you financially secure. And, leaders are **rare**.

Ask a network marketer if he has leaders in his group and he'll reply,

"Oh yeah, sure I do. I've got a few really good people."

Here's the misconception.

"Really good people" are **not** leaders. They are **only** "really good people."

A leader is much more than a good worker, a good recruiter, a good producer.

A network marketing leader is somebody who ...

* gets the most out of new distributors and helps them become more than they can become alone.

* will make sure his or her distributors order products at the end of the month.

* never complains to downline distributors.

* never complains or whines to the upline sponsor or to the company.

* has his or her own goals and aspirations.

* conducts the regular opportunity meeting for you when you are away.

* makes sure the hotel room is taken care of, the product display is set up, and the meeting starts on time.

* is in personal control of his attitude and doesn't let outside influences control his success.

* sets a strong personal example of a steady focus on the ultimate goal.

* is happy when you're gone, so he or she can do their business peacefully without your interference while enjoying taking responsibility and being in control.

There's so much more than the above, but you get the idea. Leaders are rare! Very, very rare!

How rare?

Counting real leaders.

Well, if you have one real leader in your group, you are financially fortunate.

If you have two real leaders in your group, you are very rich — independently wealthy.

If you have **three, four,** or **five** real leaders in your group, **you probably miscounted!**

Leaders are just that rare.

Leaders are how you measure your success in network marketing.

Distributors come and go, sort of like sand washing on and off the beach. They don't have that 100% commitment to their networking business.

Distributors think:

"Well, I'll try this company for a while, and then maybe I'll try this company for a while, then maybe I'll watch television for a while, and if the bonus check is too small, I will quit."

Distributors have spent their whole lives learning to quit.

They quit school, they quit their jobs, they quit exercising, they quit their New Year's resolutions, they quit their marriages, they quit their diets.

Let's face it.

Most people are professional quitters. (Now, that is not entirely bad. Quitting our job or quitting watching television at night might be appropriate.)

Since these people come and go, you can't build your group strictly on distributors. You need leaders.

Disasters?

If the press unfairly reports on your business, you might lose some uncommitted distributors.

If a temporary product shortage occurs, more distributors will retire to mindless browsing of the Internet and watching cable television.

If the company adjusts a few policies and procedures, a few more distributors will exit because they fear change in their lives.

However, none of these disasters will affect your leaders. Your leaders will continue to recruit, build, and motivate their downlines.

Okay. Having one or even two leaders may sound really great, but how do you build or find these rare, motivated, loyal potential leaders?

You will want to locate a potential leader who works so well in your absence, that you'll have plenty of time to build a second leader.

The counterfeit leader syndrome.

Some people think they have leaders or potential leaders, but they really don't.

Back in the early 80s, a couple of large network marketing companies went out of business. Some of their distributors had over 50,000 people in their downlines.

Since their network marketing company was defunct, many of these "leaders" with large organizations went looking for another networking opportunity.

They would approach a distributor with another company and say:

"I'm looking for a sponsor to get into your network marketing company. I'd like to join your company. I just came from this network marketing company that went out of business and I had 50,000 folks in my group."

The sponsor got all excited:

"Wow, this guy's going to join. He has 50,000 distributors in his group. I'm going to be rich. I'm going to retire. I'm going to Hawaii!"

Maybe to Hawaii by slow freighter.

So the "leader" joins. What the sponsor didn't realize is that the group didn't really have loyalty to this so-called "leader." He never really helped them. He didn't do any favors for them. There was no relationship.

Out of the 50,000 people in his organization, 40,000 retired from network marketing. They didn't want anything more to do with it.

Out of the remaining 10,000, about 9,000 of them didn't even know this so-called "leader" existed.

Out of the remaining 1,000, about 950 knew and hated this so-called "leader."

Out of the remaining 50 distributors, about 45 just weren't sure if they wanted to join.

That left only five people out of the original 50,000 downline who were willing to sign up.

Here is this "great leader" who really had only about five distributors. That is not a leader!

Finding those rare leaders.

Distributors come and go, but leaders are the people who are loyal to you and the company.

They are working the business for their own reasons. They'll continue working their business when you are in Hawaii or on a Caribbean cruise.

How do you get that loyalty? How do you find a leader like that?

Many newer distributors will see a leader in a different, competitive network marketing company. He's doing really well.

The new distributor thinks:

"Maybe if I make this leader a really great offer, I can steal him from his upline. He will quit his present company and come join my opportunity instead. Yeah, let me offer him an extra $500 a month more than he is making now."

Sounds good in theory. Why not just bribe a leader over to your group? If he isn't loyal to his present sponsor and company right now, this should be pretty easy.

Sounds good, but there's just one little problem.

What is going to happen when your new, freshly stolen and bribed leader gets another offer that is just a little bit better than yours?

Let's say someone else offers this leader $501 extra a month. Whoops! Your "stolen" leader has just been stolen by someone else.

Look at it this way. You just can't go around stealing leaders, because if they aren't loyal to their present sponsors, they certainly won't be loyal to you.

Obviously, this method isn't for us. How about something else?

Another approach.

What you need to do is find someone who is not a leader, someone who is dedicated and wants to learn this business.

You tell this potential leader,

"If you're really sincere, and you really want to do this business, I'm going to make you successful. I'm going to work, work, work, and work with you, teach you what you need to know to become a leader, and continue until we build you a solid group and a full-time income."

Imagine you spend six months helping to make this person successful. Do you believe your newly-developed leader thinks highly of you and your commitment to his success? He sure does. He will think you are the greatest thing since sliced bread and cable television. He might even consider having a picture of you on his desk next to his family.

Now, what happens six months from now, when another distributor approaches your new leader and says:

"Hey, quit where you are now. Come with me, start all over again from scratch, come join my new, wonderful network marketing opportunity. I know you don't know me, and I just contacted you now, and I don't normally steal leaders from other groups, but I'll be around to help you. Trust me."

Your leader will think, "Hey, if this person is okay with stealing people from others, this person will probably end up stealing people from me!"

Your leader might tactfully reply to this person by saying:

"I don't know much about you. I do know that I can't be successful jumping around to different network marketing opportunities. And I do know that my sponsor invested six months to make me successful. I wasn't successful before, now I am. I owe some loyalty to my sponsor. Plus I know my sponsor is going to continue to work with me. He's not just going to give me some lip service or promises."

You have security with leaders whom you personally build. You can sleep at night. You won't be worried about network marketing pirates bearing bribes.

That's how you protect your business so that you are constantly building and going forward on a sound foundation. Nobody likes working hard just to replace lost leaders and lost business.

That's one of the keys of network marketing superstars. They **build** and **keep** their leaders.

Real duplication.

About 35 years ago, a stranger came to me and said he wanted to be successful in network marketing. He said,

"I want to really go for it. I want to be a top leader."

Well, over the next six months we practically lived together. We worked together at every available opportunity. We traveled together. We did two-on-one presentations and opportunity meetings together. We gave training meetings together. We prospected together. And guess what?

After six months, this new leader knew everything I knew.

Duplication?

No.

It was better than that.

You see, my new leader knew everything I knew, **plus** he had all his own personal experience and wisdom. He was the product of my knowledge plus his own unique personal knowledge.

Yes, he was an even better leader than I was.

Now, this is no time to get jealous or upset. How many people would love to have some personally-sponsored leaders who are even more talented than themselves? This definitely is not the time to let one's ego get out of hand, because we're talking money — serious money. It is great to have super-talented leaders on your team.

Better than real duplication? Absolutely!

After I trained my new leader to be better than myself, guess what he did?

He immediately started mentoring his first potential leader. For the next 18 months he trained his new emerging leader. Now, what did this new leader know after the 18-month apprenticeship?

First, he knew everything I knew.

Second, he knew everything his sponsor knew.

Third, he also knew everything he personally knew from his own experience.

This new leader knew more and was a better producer than his sponsor was or I was. He was better at network marketing than both of us — and he made a point of constantly reminding both of us of that fact. And that is okay.

Now, in a period of less than three years, I had developed two good solid leaders who were more talented than I was. Yes, I was happy.

Wouldn't you be?

Intelligence test.

Now, compare the following two scenarios.

Scenario #1: You work hard for three years, sponsoring lots and lots of distributors. You give plenty of opportunity meetings, solve downline social problems, change companies once or twice — and at the end of three years you have nothing.

Scenario #2: You develop one or two leaders over three years, and become rich, retired, secure, and very, very happy.

Hmmm, not a very tough choice.

It's the steady, slow, focused network marketing leaders **who build one leader at a time** who really maximize the benefits of a networking career. They have the patience and the vision that this is a lifelong career, not a job.

Lifelong career?

Of course. We all do network marketing every day, we might as well get paid for it!

Sorting for potential leaders.

Yes, always think in terms of leaders. All along in your career you're going to be sponsoring distributors.

However, occasionally you are going to see somebody who says,

"Hmmm, maybe I can be a leader, too."

Helping this person become a leader will require a lot of work and a lot of time. We can't afford to spend six months or one year with a pseudo-leader. We want to be almost certain this potential leader prospect is serious.

After all, who wants to waste six months of his life on an unqualified prospect? That would be six months of your life that you would never get back. Time is a valuable asset.

The sincerity test.

How can we test for sincerity and commitment? Here's one way.

Ask your potential leader,

"How do you feel about this business?"

Then listen.

There are three types of commitment. Pay close attention. It could save you months and months of wasted time.

The first commitment is when a prospect says, **"Well, I'll try."** This is the weakest form of commitment. This is the commitment that creates temporary distributors.

The second type of commitment is when the prospect announces, **"I'll do the best that I can."** This is much better. Many of our best distributors make this commitment.

Finally, there is the third type of commitment when the prospect promises, **"I'll do whatever it takes."** Our potential sales leaders will make this type of commitment. And this is only their first step. It will take a lot more for them to actually become a leader. But if they are unwilling to make this first step, you might want to save your time for someone who deserves and needs your time more.

So imagine your distributor answers,

"This business sounds pretty good. I'm ready to give it a **try**."

When your distributor says that he will try it, what does that mean?

Does it mean if he doesn't get a check tomorrow, or if the check is not directly deposited in his bank, he'll quit? Does it mean he is going to work for a few weeks, and if he is not lucky, he'll try something else? Maybe he'll try the state lottery?

Your distributor is saying this:

"I'll try it, it seems to be convenient. It doesn't appear to require much work."

Press a little harder for a commitment and you'll hear this distributor say:

"Are you telling me I actually have to go to opportunity meetings? I already know how they end! And use the product? Why should I have to use the product? I just want to sell it."

Or,

"Why do I have to go to training? I just want to be rich. Isn't there a shortcut?"

Basically, we are talking about a distributor here with the lowest level of commitment. This is not a potential leader.

A better commitment.

Let's ask another distributor,

"How do you feel about this business?"

Then listen.

He replies,

"I'll do my best."

Pretty good commitment, isn't it? You would like one of your distributors to approach you and say:

"Yes! I want to be a leader. And, you have my commitment that I will do my very best!"

And do you know what? This distributor will do his very best. Now, if his best isn't good enough to make it to the top, to become a leader, what happens?

Your distributor says,

"Well, I did my best. I gave it my best shot. It just didn't work out."

It just didn't work out???

Ouch!

That's not what you want to hear after a six-month investment in your "potential" leader.

He gave his best effort. He worked hard. That is a pretty good commitment, but that **didn't** make him a leader.

What you actually had was a really good distributor.

Nothing wrong with that.

We all love good, committed distributors. But the commitment level of "I'll do my best," is not enough for you to **risk** six months of day-to-day mentoring.

You are going to want an even higher commitment before you take on a "leader trainee."

Real commitment.

Let's ask another potential leader,

"How do you feel about this business?"

Then listen.

He replies,

"I will do whatever it takes!"

Now **that's** the kind of commitment you are looking for.

This is the kind of commitment that can withstand hurricanes of negativity, and the rejection of friends, relatives, and co-workers. This potential leader will respond to challenges with the spirit of total commitment to his goal.

When a bunch of friends say "No," he simply says to himself,

"Well, I will just talk to some more people."

When his entire warm market rejects him, he says,

"Maybe I need to do some more work on my presentation and communication skills."

When competitors try to steal your potential leader into their programs, he says,

"It is not your program or my program that will make me rich. It is my personal effort and effectiveness that will make me rich. I'm staying with my mentor until I succeed."

What a difference a total commitment can make! These are the rare individuals we like to invest in to develop them into true leaders.

Remember, it only takes one leader to make you "financially fortunate."

And if you develop two leaders, then you're rich beyond your wildest imagination. And if you think you have three, four or even five leaders, well, you probably miscounted. Leaders are rare.

So don't spend two years or even twenty years treading water. You will just be exhausted, you will just be frustrated, and you will never make any permanent progress in your business.

Instead, invest your precious time in network marketing into developing **leaders**.

Where do I find leaders?

And, how do I develop them? What do I teach them? Important questions.

Everyone wishes for a massive organization and more leaders in their group. Life would be wonderful. The bonus checks would be too heavy to carry. And, we could watch cable television 24 hours a day.

So why not take a shortcut to build your network marketing business? The fastest way to build a large organization is through the help of leaders.

We can't build a very large network organization on our own if we only sponsor distributors. Our time is limited. We can only service so many distributors and their problems. Even the best distributors need some service and help.

The way to multiply our efforts is to **create** leaders who can take care of their own groups. Duplicating ourselves by creating new leaders is the only way to build a large, massive organization.

Then where do we begin?

First, let's define the difference between a network marketing leader and a distributor.

Distributors are temporary. They come and go in our business. Sometimes they work hard and build groups, and other times they may continue as a wholesale user of the product, or even quit. And it is okay that distributors are temporary. They should have the right to come and take what they want out of our business.

For instance, here are some things distributors want from our business:

* The ability to save on their personal purchases.

* A chance to make retail sales and profits.

* A feeling of belonging to a positive group of people.

* A chance to develop personally.

* Some quick checks to pay off the VISA bill.

* A part-time income to put a child through college.

* Car payments.

* Enough money for that one dream vacation.

All of these are great reasons to be a distributor. We should support and service our distributors to reach these goals. However, the truth is that this support and service should only take 10% to 20% of our time. Why?

Because distributors don't want or need a lot of support.

Some distributors say:

"Oh, don't keep calling me about those opportunity meetings. And I'm not interested in those training meetings, either. Call me when the president comes to town, or if the company introduces a new product. Otherwise, leave me alone."

Again, that is okay. We only want to help distributors get what they want out of our business. We don't want to push **our agenda** on them. They will appreciate that we respect them as adults and let them choose their own goals.

But remember, your distributors only have a temporary commitment. When the newspaper writes an unflattering article about your company, your distributor might leave. Or when the home office forgets to return the distributor's phone call, again, the distributor might quit. Or maybe a little bit of rejection from prospects will quickly end your distributor's career.

Distributors come and go, but leaders are the real thing.

Okay, we all know that leaders are more important than distributors. Most distributors are temporary and have a temporary commitment toward your business - and that's not bad. Like all of us, they're going to take what they want and then get on with their lives.

But leaders are going to stay with you and your business for a long time. So which would you rather have?

One leader or 100 distributors?

That's easy for us to answer. One leader! However, you might be thinking:

"Yeah, having one leader is great, but maybe 100 distributors would give me some pretty good bonus checks."

The problem is that we'll have to **replace** those 100 distributors as time goes on, and instead of building this residual income that we talk about, we end up with just a full-time job replacing distributors.

When we focus on leaders, it changes how we build our business.

People always ask me:

"What is the secret to success in network marketing?"

I have a quick, short answer that I have used for years. You probably remember it from the beginning of this book.

"To be successful in network marketing, all you have to do is build leaders and make them successful."

In other words, if you had a choice to go out and do a retail party to sell some skin care or vitamins or whatever, that is nice - but that is probably a job. That is not building the type of residual income you want.

While this activity is part of your business, this activity will not be the fastest route to your goal of becoming a leader.

You have to think differently if you're going to build a large and successful downline organization. You are going to carefully focus on **which** activities you do, because you want to be a leader quickly.

I will show you the difference.

Many years ago, I flew over to England to start a downline. I arrived and a friend of mine, John Church, met me at the airport. Because I had a relationship with John, he had already committed to becoming a distributor – even though he had no details.

As I walk off my plane, John is waiting for me. He has his first prospect with him, a man named Brian. Well, I gave a horrible, jet-lagged presentation and Brian joined. He didn't join because of my presentation. He joined because he was a friend of John Church.

Relationships **do** make a difference.

John Church and I then proceeded to drive towards his home so I could get a bit of sleep. Before we arrive at John's home, his mobile telephone rings. It's his new distributor, Brian.

Brian says:

"I have a contact about eight hours away in Scotland and I would like it if you could go talk to him. I just hung up the telephone with him and he said he may or may not be interested – but he would take a look at the business if you'd drive up to meet him. He will come two hours closer if you will drive the other six hours."

John looked at me and said:

"Eight hours?"

I replied:

"Tell Brian that it's **no problem**. We're on our way - just give us directions."

Well, I didn't get that nap I wanted. Instead, John and I just kept on driving to Scotland. Along the way, John said:

"Are we crazy? We're driving six hours for someone who might not even show up!"

I said:

"That's OK."

John gasped:

"What do you mean, it's okay? Six hours up and six hours back and this semi-committed prospect might not even show up!"

I explained my position:

"John, we're not going there to give a presentation. We're going there to **support** Brian. We want to let Brian know that because he wants to be a leader, we're going to help him to the ends of the earth **no matter what**, until he becomes a leader. It's irrelevant whether this prospect shows up or not. It is no big deal. We are driving six hours to show our commitment to Brian."

That is the difference in focus I'm talking about. Because we're focused on building a leader, our activity changes also. We will concentrate on different tasks and take different viewpoints on situations than other networkers, because we're building leaders.

The above example with Brian and John will also change how you feel about failure when somebody doesn't show up at a meeting, or a lot of guests don't come. You will have less stress and more focus because you're thinking:

"The reason I am doing this meeting is to develop this person into a leader."

This helps us focus on what we're doing because we know **why** we are doing our present activity. This focus and understanding helps us move forward in our business, and we make progress.

So that is what I mean by **changing what you do** to build leaders instead of lots of less important activities which can take up our day.

Now, earlier I asked if you would rather have one leader instead of 100 distributors. I am sure you chose "one leader."

But just in case you are still skeptical, consider the following example.

Generals make a difference.

Imagine that you are the supreme dictator of your own country. That's a pretty good job, and you have your own army with five loyal generals. You also have 100,000 infantry men. (Of course, the generals represent leaders and the infantry men represent distributors, in case you're not following this analogy.)

What happens next is that one night, I sneak across enemy lines and attack your army. I use my pink belt in karate and go chop, chop, chop and I beat up all 100,000 of your infantry men.

The next morning you wake up and you have five generals remaining. All of your infantry men went home to their mothers for sympathy.

Now, here's the important question.

With only five generals left, could you rebuild your army?

Of course you could. That's the importance of leaders. When things go bad and everyone abandons ship, you can still rebuild your organization if you have loyal leaders.

What if the opposite happened?

What if I were to sneak across enemy lines and kidnap your five generals? What would happen then?

The next morning, you wake up and all you have remaining are your 100,000 infantry men with no leadership or direction. They start marching in circles, firing inward, stepping in latrines, and getting lost. It's a disaster!

So as you see, generals are everything.

Some networkers build leaders.
Other networkers are just busy.

That explains why some networkers can work for a few years and finally retire from their business. These networkers focused all their activity on building leaders.

The other networkers? The ones that were just busy? Well, they're still busy.

If you're not convinced that building leaders is important by now ... well, I don't know what else I could say.

Okay! Okay! Let's get some leaders!

We need a step-by-step plan. And that's easy because I studied engineering. If you are not familiar with engineers, we need a step-by-step plan for everything. That is why we find it hard to dance without blueprints and instructions, and no one has given us the complete rulebook on matching clothing. Thus, our fashion tastes are ... different.

For instance, when engineers walk, we have a plan. We're thinking:

"Left foot, then the right foot. Left foot, then the right foot, etc."

Anyway, back to our detailed plan. We are going to create our master plan in three easy steps. By mastering each step, one step at a time, we'll end up with an organization of leaders.

Here are the steps to master:

Step #1: Define what a leader is.

Step #2: How to find leaders.

Step #3: What to teach leaders.

Step #1: Define what a leader is.

Before we go looking for leaders, wouldn't it be a great idea to know **what a leader looks like?**

It is a lot easier to find somebody if we know what he looks like.

On a recent teleconference training call, I asked the group:

"Does anybody on tonight's call have a good definition of what is a leader is?"

The answers were:

* Someone who is willing to step up and help encourage others.

* Someone who makes sure that he gets done what needs to be done.

* Somebody who is coachable.

* Somebody who is good with people - a good communicator.

* Someone with a vision.

* Someone who wants to learn and wants to succeed.

* Someone who commits to taking the action that is required to make it to the top.

And that was the list. The rest of the callers were silent. I don't think they ever thought about this question. I can't imagine how they looked for leaders if they never even knew what a leader looked like.

What is my definition of a leader?

I have **three** definitions of a leader. These aren't the only three definitions. They're not all-inclusive. These are just three starting definitions to give us an idea of what we are looking for.

The first definition I heard is from a man named Tracy Dietrich in Dallas, Texas. He says that leaders are:

Professional students of the business.

In other words, leaders actually read the sales manual that came with their distributor kit. By this definition, everybody reading this book would be a leader. We are students of network marketing – always looking for new ideas and information.

Leaders listen to audio trainings, read books, go to meetings and, whenever they can, they attend company conventions. You'll see leaders hanging around with the active leaders hoping to pick up a good idea.

I like this definition. It makes it easy to spot leaders. Just go to any training meeting and you will see the chairs full of leaders. Leaders want to learn.

Sounds good, but what is my second definition of a leader?

This definition is a little harder to explain but easy to **observe.**

Imagine that you decide to take a vacation to Hawaii. You are going to miss your local weekly opportunity meeting. Somebody will have to conduct your weekly meeting.

A leader conducts the opportunity meeting, makes sure the product display is there, pays for the room, and assumes the responsibility to make sure that everything runs smoothly. **And you don't have to call from Hawaii to see if it was done.**

In other words, you're on vacation and you don't have to worry or check on anything. This leader was **glad** you left town so he could take the responsibility!

This is a pretty good definition of a leader. He is someone who does his business without your constant motivation and checking. He is someone you don't have to worry about.

The third definition of a leader is the toughest.

This definition separates the so-called leaders from the real leaders. Here it is:

A leader is someone who handles **problems.**

Let's say there is a problem in the downline. Mike didn't get his order or Mary talked longer than Al or there was some bad news in the local press, or whatever.

A leader handles the problem.

Your leader will call the home office to trace the order, will help Al understand why Mary talked longer, or support and counsel a devastated distributor who is upset over some bad publicity.

The leadership test is this:

Will the problem filter upline to you?

If you have a distributor who you think is a leader - but the distributor is still passing problems up to you, this distributor doesn't qualify to be a leader.

This is a tough test, but it separates leaders from the crowd.

Now we have three clear descriptions of a leader. We know exactly what we are searching for.

Now that we have a really good grip on what a leader is, the next question in your mind should be:

Step #2: How do I find leaders?

Step #2: How do I find leaders?

That's simple.

There are only two ways to get leaders.

The first way to get leaders is to **steal** them. We talked about that earlier, how a new distributor thinks:

"Maybe if I make this leader a really great offer, I can steal him from his upline. He will quit his present company and come join my opportunity instead. Yeah, let me offer him an extra $500 a month more than he is making now."

Ouch!

If this leader can be bought once, this leader can be bought again.

So we could steal leaders, but the problem is that we will only end up with **temporary** leaders. This means we would have a job for the rest of our lives replacing leader after leader, wouldn't we? This isn't what we're looking for.

You see, a lot of distributors advertise for leaders. They try to persuade leaders to join them with the newest hot deal because it costs a tenth of a cent less or it pays 1% more. But what happens when someone else charges two-tenths of a cent less or pays 2% more?

The temporary leader is gone.

Plus, leaders usually aren't sitting around the house, unemployed, answering ads from desperate sponsors. They are not waiting. They are out doing something.

It is a full-time job replacing temporary leaders. It's not really building a permanent, loyal network marketing organization.

Let's save time and eliminate further discussion about stealing leaders because that's not really what we want to do. We want permanent income.

So what is the second way to get leaders?

The second way to get leaders is to **build them from scratch.**

In other words, we are going to find a distributor who is **not** a leader now. Then, we're going to **teach** him exactly **how** to become a leader.

But there is a challenge!

If this distributor is **not** a leader now, he is going to look **exactly** like any other temporary distributor, right? So what does a leader look like?

Profile of a leader.

At a leadership event, I asked all the leaders to stand up, look around at the other leaders, and see how many of the other leaders were like them.

After looking around, the leaders couldn't find anyone else like themselves.

The lesson?

Don't spend too much time trying to get people to be like you, to act like you, to do exactly the same things that you do, etc.

It is okay to have leaders who are not carbon copies of yourself. Allow them the freedom to conduct their business their way.

One "system" will not fit everyone. Having a system is great. Most new distributors want a system. Just remember that one size doesn't fit everyone.

So what do we look for?

How do we know who to build into a leader? How do we avoid wasting time building the wrong person who will never become a leader?

Have you ever worked with someone who is coachable, committed to action, wanted to be a leader -- and that person **never** became a leader? Has that ever happened to you? Have you experienced the wasted time and effort?

Well, I spent my first 15 years in network marketing with this same frustration.

I did this. I said:

"If you want to be a leader, let's go for it."

I practically moved in with the committed distributor. We drove all over the country together. We made phone calls together. We gave meetings together. I taught the distributor everything I knew.

And most of the time, he didn't become a leader.

I ended up wasting a lot of my time. The distributor wasted a lot of his time. And nothing permanent was accomplished.

That all changed when I met a guy named Tom Paredes. He came up to me and said this:

"Big Al, you're an idiot."

Of course this immediately got my attention. I said to myself:

"I better listen to this guy. He is right. He is telling the truth. I have been wasting all this time working hard – but training the wrong people."

Tom Paredes continued. He said:

"If you're going to train everybody who **says** that he wants to be a leader, it is not going to work. Talk is cheap."

Well, I asked the obvious question:

"So how do you know who to train and who not to train? Everyone wants to be a leader. They told me so. How do you know which one to work with?"

Tom Paredes answered:

"You simply give them a test."

I smacked my forehead. I had just wasted fifteen years! Why hadn't I given these candidates a test? Well, because ... I never thought of it. There is an old saying that goes like this:

"Don't believe what people say, only observe what they **do**."

And now that I knew that I should give the candidates a test, what would be my next obvious question?

You're right! What kind of test should I give them?

Again Tom Paredes had a simple answer. He said:

"You give them a book! Tell them to read the book and that you'll check back with them in three days to discuss the book."

Now it all made sense.

Imagine that you were in a business and you sponsored me. I said that I wanted to learn how to become a leader, so you tell me:

"Big Al, here is a book that is really going to help you build your business. I know you want to be a leader. Today is Monday. Why don't we get together on Thursday and discuss what is in this book? I will show you how you can use the principles in this book in your business."

Of course I will thank you for the book and say that I'm looking forward to our Thursday meeting. Well, Thursday comes and you call me.

I start making excuses over the telephone and say:

"Well, I couldn't read the book on Monday, because that's when Monday Night Football comes on television. And then on Tuesday, I had to work overtime on my job. Wednesday night is family night. That's when the family goes out and I can watch television in peace. So I really haven't read the book yet."

What would that tell you about me?

That says:

"Hey, if I can't put forth enough effort to read the book, what chance is there that I would put forth an effort to take guests to meetings? To go to other trainings and listen to audios? To drive to conventions? To put up with problems and challenges on my way to the top?"

This doesn't mean that I will always be a non-leader. It just means that at this time in my life, I am not willing to make a commitment. It doesn't mean I am a terrible person, it just means that, hey, I'm not going to put forth the effort to learn to be a leader right now.

It is important that we give this test **before** we invest time in training a distributor to become a leader. If we don't perform this test, any time that we spend with an uncommitted distributor is wasted.

We may be stealing time from somebody who desperately needs to be a leader.

But what happens if you give me a book and the next morning I give you a call at 6 a.m.?

I say:

"I know it is early, but I am wired with excitement. I have highlighted the book and made an outline. I know it's 6 a.m., but let's get together for breakfast. If we hurry up, we can have breakfast at 6:30 a.m. and talk about this book before I go to work."

What would that tell you?

Ka-ching!

We have a winner here. This is a simple test but it makes all the difference in the world.

By the way, I haven't mentioned which book to give as a test, have I?

Of course, you can give them a "Big Al" book because they will learn great network marketing skills. Any of my wonderfully-written books would do.

But it doesn't matter which book you give as a test!

Why? Because it's only a test. You're only checking for **action** from your potential leader. Remember, almost everyone will **say** that they want to become a leader, but talk is cheap. You have to check for that action commitment.

So if you don't have a book handy, you can give them a National Geographic Magazine, right? It doesn't matter. You are only checking for action.

By the way, if you don't have a book or a magazine, what else can you give as a test?

You could use a video, an audio, or have your potential leader listen to a conference call - or send him to a store for milk and cookies. It's only a test.

But if you don't have a book, an audio, or even a video, you might reconsider **your** leadership capabilities.

Danger! Danger! Depression approaching!

When you give your potential leadership candidates this test, I have to give you this warning:

You might get depressed.

After reading about this test, you will want to grab a book and give this leadership test to your brother-in-law, your friends, and to your best distributors.

You might expect too much from these people.

Let me tell you a story about a friend of mine in Canada. He was doing pretty well with his business, but after he heard about this leadership test, he went out and gave this test to some of his distributors.

He called me a year later and said:

"I took your advice last year and I gave my best distributors the leadership test. I gave them all a book. Here's what happened. All of my so-called potential leaders – **flunked!** I felt really bad and totally depressed.

"Then, here is what I did next. I gave this same test to a bunch of second-stringers. You know, the people who didn't drive as nice a car, didn't have as many contacts, didn't have as big of a vocabulary, didn't seem like the salesmen – just ordinary distributors who weren't quite as good as my top people.

"Again, most of those second-stringers failed. However, a few of these distributors passed the test, and I have spent the last year working with them. It has been the most productive year of my life!

"I don't have to call these people to make sure they're coming to meetings. **They call me** to make sure that I am going to be there. We have the most positive people at our opportunity meetings - people who are motivated, people who are going places. It has been a fantastic year!"

The reason I tell you this story is **not** because it has a happy ending.

I tell this story because here is what will happen after you read this book.

You'll give this leadership test to a lot of your best distributors and most of them are going to flunk. And then you'll say:

"I know my brother-in-law would really, really make a great leader and the only reason he didn't read the book is ..."

And you'll start making up excuses for people who aren't ready to become a leader.

Then, you'll start investing time with really nice people who didn't pass the leadership test – and won't become leaders. Bad for business.

So be prepared for some disappointment. Don't take the results personally. You are only looking for distributors who pass the test and are willing to invest action to back up their words.

Don't invest leadership training time with distributors who don't pass the test.

Let me give you an example of the conversations you will have with distributors who don't pass the leadership test.

***

Distributor: I've been working this business for three months now and I'm just not making any money. This business doesn't work.

Big Al: Strange. This business seems to work for some. And if this business works for some, and doesn't work for others, then maybe the business isn't what makes the difference. There must be some other factor.

Distributor: Well, the products are too expensive. That's why I can't make this business work.

Big Al: Strange. I think that everyone in our company has the same products. I don't think any of the leaders get a special set of products with special prices. The leaders get the same products as the other distributors. Hmmm. I don't think the products are what make a difference in your business.

Distributor: If the compensation plan paid better, it would be easier to get prospects to join. Why doesn't the company pay out more money on personal enrollments?

Big Al: Strange. I think the leaders have the same compensation plan as the other distributors.

Distributor: So what are you trying to say? Are you saying that it is my fault? Are you accusing me of not being a leader?

Big Al: Well, let's see. Is it okay if I ask you a few questions about how you are attempting to build your business?

Distributor: Sure. Go ahead.

Big Al: When you give presentations to prospects, do you know the three reasons why prospects make the decision to join?

Distributor: Uh, three reasons? Well, I guess I really don't know that one. I am not sure what the three reasons are that determine the prospects' decisions.

Big Al: When talking with prospects, do you address the three questions prospects need to know in order to make an intelligent decision to join or not to join?

Distributor: Three important questions, huh? No, I don't think I am familiar with them. Maybe I don't answer those questions in my presentation.

Big Al: When you give a presentation, what is the first sentence you use to get the prospect to lean forward instead of leaning back?

Distributor: Well, I kind of make it up as I go. I am not really sure what first sentence to use to get the prospects interested. But it really doesn't matter. I don't have that many appointments or presentations anyway.

Big Al: Not many presentations, eh? Then what two sentences do you use to get an appointment? If you use the right two sentences, you can get an appointment with almost 100% of the people you talk to.

Distributor: Okay, I don't have a clue. Maybe that is why I can't get appointments for a presentation.

Big Al: You meet someone at a party. You think they might be a great prospect for your business. What simple, eight-word question can you ask that will build trust?

Distributor: Don't know.

Big Al: What seven-word question will create an interested prospect on demand?

Distributor: I guess maybe I might do better if I knew what to say and do.

Big Al: Where is the best place to find good prospects?

Distributor: I wish I knew where to find good prospects.

Big Al: How can you turn neutral prospects into good prospects?

Distributor: No idea.

***

And so the conversation went.

Frustrating, isn't it. A distributor wants to earn big bonus checks, but won't invest the time and energy to learn the skills necessary to earn the big bonus checks.

And here is the sad, sad part of this conversation.

All of the answers to the questions I asked were on the training CDs I **loaned** him two months earlier!

Instead of learning what to do, this distributor failed the leadership test and watched television, made a few unsuccessful prospecting calls, and convinced himself that "the business doesn't work."

Well, he is right. "The business doesn't work."

We work.

I did a poor job of covering this important fact with the new distributor when he joined. He is not totally to blame. It is hard to know "what you don't know."

Someone has to make distributors aware of what they don't know. That is just one of our jobs as a leader. We can't assume that new prospects know everything they need to learn and master to become successful.

But, before you invest that time in training, make sure that distributor passed the leadership test first.

You can run with 1,000 leaders, but you can only drag ... one!

We can't build a huge team without leaders. And we can't build leaders if we are dragging people with us every step of the way.

Let's move on. We have given our distributors the leadership test and identified people **who look like** ordinary distributors, **who act like** ordinary distributors, but these are special people. These chosen few will now be **trained** to become leaders.

Here's the $64,000 Question!

Remember Step #3? Well, if you don't, let me review these three logical steps.

Step #1: Define what a leader is.

We have three definitions. This step is easy.

Step #2: How to find leaders.

We just covered this. Sure, we can find leaders, but they'll be temporary leaders. The permanent way to build leaders is to train ordinary distributors (who pass the leadership test) to become leaders.

Step #3: What to teach leaders.

Yes, this is the big question! What do leaders know that distributors **don't** know?

Why not look into that right now?

Step #3: What to teach leaders.

Look at it this way. You have taught your new distributor to be a good distributor - and that means you taught him:

* All about the products.

* All about the company.

* How to be loyal.

* How to create rapport with prospects.

* Basic "Ice Breakers" to get presentations.

* How to network.

* How to be positive.

* How to sponsor effectively.

* How to retail products.

* How to duplicate his efforts, etc., etc., etc.

After teaching your distributor all these important skills, you now have a really well-trained distributor – **but you don't have a leader!**

So now you decide you're going to teach your distributor to become a leader.

What are you going to teach him?

What must this distributor know that will make him a leader?

Great question!

I would like you to stop reading now and think about this question. Why? Because as busy networkers, we get so involved with building a business that we fail to stop, think, and plan exactly what we **should** be doing.

Here is your chance to plan. Write in the space below exactly what you should be teaching your potential leader. And remember, it is not any of the things we just listed above.

```



```

If you are like most people I talk to, you **didn't** write anything in the above space.

Now, I am not sadistic, but I love asking this question. Everywhere I travel throughout the world, I ask the question:

"Now that you've taught your distributor to be a good distributor, how to be positive, how to duplicate, etc., **what** are you going to teach him so that he learns to become a leader?"

And the answer is usually dead silence.

People just stare blankly into space or stare like a deer into an oncoming automobile's headlights. This question paralyzes networkers because we never think about how to really develop leaders.

Here is what many networkers do to attempt to build a distributor into a leader.

They teach their distributor to be positive.

That's nice, but all they create is a more positive distributor.

Or, they move in with their distributor.

That was my original, very flawed plan.

All their waking hours are spent teaching new skills to the distributor. They travel with the new distributor. They do presentations with the new distributor. They attend training seminars and regional conventions with the new distributor.

That's nice.

The leaders bond and build a relationship with their new distributor. However, all they accomplish is developing a really **friendly** distributor. Having friends is a great thing. But wouldn't it be nice to build a leader or two so that we could have enough money to spend more time with our good friends?

But it gets worse.

Do distributors waste your time?

Has this ever happened to you? Have you said to yourself:

"This distributor would make a great leader. I'm going to travel with him, help him become positive, and train him with everything I know."

And what happens?

Most times it doesn't work out. All of our training and effort is wasted. Our distributor does not become a leader. Worse yet, he may even quit our business.

And there you have it. Six months, a year, or even more of our time – wasted!

All of our time and effort -- and **nothing to show for it.** Not only did we waste our time, but we wasted our distributor's time, too.

Could we be teaching the wrong things?

In order to know what to teach distributors to build them into leaders ... we first must identify the true difference between leaders and distributors. What is the difference?

* Are leaders taller?

* More handsome or more beautiful?

* Live in better neighborhoods?

* Drive different types of cars?

* Memorize presentations more accurately?

* Have outgoing personalities only?

* Self-starters?

* More focused and driven?

Here is the real difference.

The only difference between leaders and distributors is:

How they think!

In every situation or problem, a leader will think **differently** than a distributor.

Aha! So if we can train our distributor to think **differently** when problems, challenges, or situations arise ... then we will have a better-trained leader. Great!

How are we going to do this?

We will make a list of problems, challenges, and situations and write down:

1. How a distributor would think, and

2. How a leader would think.

Once we have completed our list, we will start training our potential leader, the person who passed the original leadership test. When a problem, challenge, or situation arises, we'll take our potential leader aside and say:

"There are two ways to think about this - as a leader and as a distributor. Let me show you the difference."

Then we will methodically explain the difference between the two ways of thinking.

A potential leader can't learn what he doesn't know.

We must give him the knowledge so he can learn this new way of thinking.

If we don't do this, your potential leader will never develop, will flounder aimlessly, and will attempt to learn and memorize all kinds of nice information that won't help him to become a leader. Your potential leader will become frustrated!

Here's what happened to me. Back in 1974, I'd been in the business for a few years and desperately wanted to be a leader. A famous leader with our company came to town and said:

"I'm going to show all of you how to become leaders."

Now, I am excited. So there I am sitting in the front row - well, actually I am in the second row because I don't want to be called on or volunteered for anything.

The famous leader tells our group this:

"If you want to be a leader, be more positive."

I'm sitting there thinking:

"Could you be a little more specific? That doesn't help me at all. There is nothing tangible that I can grasp. I have been trained to be a good employee all my life. My teachers told me to get a good job. My employer says to work hard and I can get promoted to a better job. I think like an employee and you have to tell me **exactly** what to do."

I left that meeting pretty frustrated. I didn't get the knowledge and information I needed to change. The worst part was that **I didn't know what to change** in order to become a leader.

Do your potential leaders suffer the same frustration?

If they do, let's solve their frustration and teach them exactly **how** and **what** to think in every problem, challenge, or situation.

The best way to show you how this works is to give you some practical, everyday examples that you can use right away. Let's get started.

Imagine that you sell a product. You go next door and sell some product to your neighbor. You come back home, order the product from the home office and … it's on backorder!

If this happened to you, what would you think? Would you think:

"This is terrible! I took my neighbor's money and didn't deliver his products. He is really going to be mad at me. And then he will tell everyone in the neighborhood that I am dishonest. My reputation will be ruined. I will never be able to show my face again. Everyone in the neighborhood is going to laugh at me. My company can't even keep the products in stock. That's a simple job. If the company can't even keep products in stock, well, they probably won't be able to pay bonus checks. They probably can't even hire and fire employees properly. In fact, I bet they don't even have employees – just a bunch of answering machines. The company is going to collapse. And Western civilization as we know it will collapse! This is terrible - I quit!"

Would you characterize this as leadership thinking or as distributor thinking?

It's obvious – this is **distributor thinking** and you would get **distributor results** and a **distributor-sized bonus check** because of this thinking.

Everyone has problems.

Leaders and distributors face the same problems every day. Leaders don't become leaders because of lack of problems. They become leaders because of how they **think** and **handle** problems.

Leadership thinking.

How would a leader think when confronted with the exact same backorder situation? A leader might think:

"Whoa, the product is backordered. These products are so much in demand that even if my customers give me money, they still can't get the product. It's so exclusive and selling so well, the company can't keep the products in stock. My new customer is going to be so impressed, he will probably order two or three times more product to make sure he can get some. That means two or three times more product volume for me, and two or three times the bonus check. Wow! I hope they bring on some more backorders - yes!"

Would you characterize this as leadership thinking or as distributor thinking?

It's obvious – this is **leadership thinking** and you would get **leadership results** and a **leader-sized bonus check** because of this thinking.

Here is what distributors don't know.

It **doesn't cost anything** to change your thinking. Most distributors think:

"Well, I am stuck with one kind of thinking. There is no way that I can change it. This is the **only** way to look at situations."

This "I can't change my thinking" viewpoint comes from years of conditioning from parents, teachers, friends, and employers. But this viewpoint isn't true.

Of course, we can all change our thinking – if we want to. But how do you convince your potential leader that he can change his thinking?

With a story.

Stories are the best way to change people's thinking. They are easy to remember, and your potential leader can see himself in the story. He can identify with the story.

To help your potential leader see that changing one's thinking is possible, try sharing a story similar to this:

Imagine that you are driving along one day and a red Ferrari automobile almost forces you off the road. The driver appears to be a young teenager and he is obviously speeding. How do you feel? What do you think about the driver?

If your potential leader answers honestly, he'll say:

"I don't like that teenager. He is reckless and I almost had an accident. Someone should report him to the police and have him arrested. He is a danger to society."

Later that day you get a call from the hospital. It's from your son. Your son says, "Hi. Just wanted to let you know that the doctors said that I'm going to be okay. I fell off my bike and suffered a serious cut. I could have bled to death, but fortunately a teenager in a red Ferrari was driving by. He picked me up and raced me to the hospital just in time."

Now, ask your potential leader this:

"What do you think about that teenage driver now?"

If your potential leader answers honestly, he will say:

"You are right. I did change my thinking, and it didn't cost me anything. The situation was the same. And you know what? I could have chosen to change my thinking about that teenage driver even if I didn't get that additional information. You are right. I can change my thinking any time I choose."

Now that your potential leader understands that he can change his thinking, you will want to teach him this.

Point out that there are two ways of thinking – leadership thinking and distributor thinking.

1. If you think like a leader you will get **leader results** and a **leader-sized bonus check.**

2. If you think like a distributor, you will get **distributor results** and a **distributor-sized bonus check.**

Then give your potential leader a big dose of personal responsibility. Tell him:

"I am **not** going to change your thinking. That is up to you. If you want distributor results, think like a distributor. If you want leadership results, think like a leader. It is strictly up to you which results you want. Pick the results you want in your life, and then you will know which type of thinking to choose."

This is a big step -- but this is the only way you effectively build a leader. Because if you don't do this, you are going to spend a lifetime fixing all their problems, answering all their questions, holding their hands, and trying to re-motivate them after every challenge.

Okay, okay. So what exactly will I teach them?

Let's make this concrete here.

First, write down all the everyday problems you encounter in your business.

Second, for each problem, write down what would represent leadership thinking and what would represent distributor thinking.

And **third**, write down any appropriate stories that you could tell your potential leader to help him change his thinking from distributor thinking to leadership thinking.

That's it. That is what you are going to have to teach them.

Teaching with stories.

Let's write down some common problems and how we'll teach our potential leader to change his thinking.

Problem #1: My sponsor doesn't help me.

Is that a common problem? I hear it all the time. People call me and complain:

"I can't become a leader. I can't even become a good distributor because my sponsor doesn't help me."

This is easy to identify as distributor thinking. Here is the story I tell the caller to help change his distributor thinking into leadership thinking.

I am a professional victim.

Here is what happened to me when I first started in network marketing. I was in business for one year and ten months and had no distributors and no retail customers. I was an absolute failure. A concerned leader came to me and say, "Big Al, you are not doing very well."

I had to defend my failure so I replied, "Of course I am not doing well. My sponsor **doesn't help me**. He doesn't know any more about this business than I do."

Then the leader stared at me and said, "Big Al, tell me about your sponsor. Did he sponsor anybody else besides you?"

Oh, oh. This was getting personal now. I had to admit that my sponsor had indeed recruited **other** distributors into the business, but most of them were not successful either. Maybe just one or two of them became successful.

And the leader closed with this cutting remark. He said:

"Big Al, tell me about the one or two other distributors who are successful. Don't they have **exactly the same sponsor** as you do?"

Ouch! That was mean!

But all of a sudden, I got it! I understood that I couldn't blame my sponsor. After all, success had nothing to do with him because he sponsored successful and unsuccessful people. And if it didn't have anything to do with the sponsor, that left ... me!

My distributor thinking instantly changed to leadership thinking because of this incident.

And when I tell this story to distributors who call, do they change their thinking that quickly also?

No.

Maybe after listening to my story, they change their thinking just a little bit – a little bit closer to leadership thinking. You might have to tell several stories over a few weeks to completely change their thinking concerning this problem.

You are not going to change someone's thinking from distributor thinking to leadership thinking overnight. However, you have to start somewhere, so why not start accumulating your stories now?

What doesn't work.

Let me tell you what I found is a complete waste of time.

Lectures.

Lectures don't work. If you want proof that lectures don't work, just think back to when you were a teenager and how many lectures you received and how well they worked.

Point made.

Lectures don't work – stories do.

So the best way to change a potential leader's thinking is with stories that illustrate graphically:

"Hey, this is reality. This is what works in the real world."

That's what happened to me when I found out that my sponsor was not the determining factor in my lack of success. I couldn't deny the facts. Other distributors had the exact same sponsor I did, and they became successful. At that moment of enlightenment, I jumped from distributor thinking all the way to leadership thinking on that one issue.

Unfortunately, I had some other issues, too. But I overcame them in exactly the same way, by recognizing a different way of thinking through the power of stories.

How about another problem?

Let's go through another concrete example of exactly how to use this method.

Imagine that my sponsor lives too far away. I can't become successful because my sponsor doesn't come to help me. How are we going to move my thinking from distributor thinking to leadership thinking?

Here's a story you could tell me.

***

You: Big Al, I know you think that you can't become successful because I live too far away. I can't help you do local meetings and I can't come to your hometown to help you do two-on-one presentations.

However, let's imagine that you're taking a flight home to Houston, Texas. There is another passenger sitting next to you on the airplane. Your casual conversation goes like this:

Big Al: Hey, what do you do for a living?

Passenger: I am the president of a local entrepreneurs' club. We have 10,000 members and they're all entrepreneurs. We meet in the evenings because we all have regular jobs, but our club is looking for a part-time business to get into.

Big Al: Oh really? What kind of business?

Passenger: Well, we don't want to have stores because that would be boring. We would be tied down to one location.

We're outgoing people and we're interested in sales and marketing. We enjoy meeting, networking, and working with other people. We don't have a lot of money to invest - maybe only a couple thousand dollars each.

But we're willing to work as hard as we can to build successful businesses.

But you know what? I haven't been able to find any part-time business for our members yet. And if I don't find something pretty soon, they're going to throw me out of office. I'm pretty worried.

You: So what are you thinking, Big Al? You're thinking, "Oh, man, I've hit the mother lode! My business opportunity is going to be perfect for her members. She is going to thank me." And then Big Al, you ask:

Big Al: Oh, by the way, where do you live?

Passenger: I live in Miami.

You: And now Big Al, you're going to throw up your hands in despair and say:

Big Al: Oh no! That's too bad. I could never sponsor you because I wouldn't be local. You can't become successful in my business unless I live close to you.

***

At that point, **I change my thinking.** I understand that if I keep believing that the sponsor must live locally, I would pass by many great opportunities. In fact, if I keep that distributor thinking, that would mean that I could never sponsor someone more than ten miles away from my house!

After you tell me that story, will my thinking move from distributor thinking to leadership thinking? Maybe not all the way, but I'm getting closer, right?

So why not tell me this story next?

The gold mine.

Imagine you are standing in a gold mine. There are hundreds and thousands of pure gold nuggets scattered at your feet (gold nuggets = opportunity, for those of you who aren't following the path of this analogy.) But, your sponsor isn't there. There is no one to tell you to pick up the gold nuggets and put them in your pocket. So, what do you do?

You go home and watch cable television because your sponsor didn't help you.

Silly, isn't it? When we join network marketing, we are provided an opportunity, not an entitlement. It is up to us to take advantage of the opportunity, or we can complain about the company's newsletter, the color of the product label, or our not-too-helpful sponsor.

So, our success in network marketing is up to us, not our sponsor. In fact, we can choose to be successful or not, even if our sponsor didn't exist.

But try this story to make things even more obvious to the distributor who still believes his sponsor must be local and helpful.

The class reunion.

Let's say you are at your class reunion. One of your old classmates says,

"Wow! You're in network marketing? That's great! I always wanted to be a network marketing distributor. Would you be my sponsor? Please? Please? I'll work harder than anybody you have ever sponsored."

Unfortunately, your classmate now lives in New York City, 500 miles away. If you believe that a distributor can't be successful unless she has a local sponsor, what are your choices?

You could sell your home and move your family to New York City so that you could be her local sponsor. But, that means you would have to move again to Chicago if you sponsored someone new there, and then to Tulsa and so on. Or what happens if your classmate moves from New York City to Florida? Does that mean you will have to move to Florida? Gets complicated, doesn't it?

So, when distributors say,

"I can't be successful because I don't have a local sponsor to help me."

Simply ask them if they are willing to move every time they sponsor a non-local distributor.

Let's do one more concrete example.

"My products are too expensive. Nobody wants to pay that much."

Sound familiar? Does this sound like distributor thinking to you?

Distributors **believe** that prospects make their buying decision based on price. Will it be hard to change their thinking?

Not if we use stories and examples.

So let's imagine that I am a potential leader, but my belief that the products are too expensive is holding me back. You want to change my thinking from:

1. "The products are too expensive."

to

2. "The products are affordable because prospects really want what they have to offer."

You take note of my distributor thinking and attempt to change my thinking, **not with a lecture**, but with the following story:

"Big Al, I know you think that the products are too expensive. You could be right. But I think a lot of people buy for convenience, quality, comfort, extra features or prestige. Most people will pay more for products when they can get this extra convenience, quality, comfort, extra features or prestige."

But I reply:

"No. I don't believe you. People buy because of price. They want to save money and will buy the least expensive products they can."

So you tell me:

"Big Al, you could be right. Maybe a lot of people go out and buy the least expensive products. I don't know. **Let's go and find out**, okay?"

You take me outside and we stand on the street corner. You ask me:

"Big Al, what's the cheapest automobile you can purchase?"

I think for a minute and say:

"A mini-Kia automobile. That's the least expensive car you can get. It has four wheels and a steering wheel and it will get you from Point A to Point B."

And then you say:

"Let's stand on this street corner. Since people buy on price, I am sure most people will purchase the least expensive automobile that they can get – a mini-Kia. I bet we will see a lot of mini-Kia automobiles drive by.

In fact, I think over 50% of the cars that will pass by us will be mini-Kia automobiles."

As we stand on that street corner, what types of automobiles pass us by? Well, first there is a Chevrolet, then a Ford, then a BMW, then a Toyota, then a Dodge, another Ford, a Cadillac, a Lexus, another Ford, a Volkswagen ... and we don't see a single mini-Kia!

You turn to me and say:

"Is it possible that people buy automobiles for prestige, comfort or quality – and not based just on price? I haven't seen a single mini-Kia yet. I don't think anybody purchases automobiles just based on price. People want image, comfort, special features, more speed, or prestige. But, hey - I could be wrong. Tell you what, let's go to another street corner. This could just be a bad location."

We walk to another street corner. What do we see?

We see Nissans, Toyotas, Fords, Chevrolets, BMWs, Mercedes, Cadillacs, and not a single mini-Kia. You turn to me and say:

"Gee, it doesn't look like anybody purchased an automobile based on price. Everybody purchased comfort, color, convenience or prestige. Let's go to another corner and look at some more automobiles."

I say:

"No, no, no. I get the point."

Again, you've changed my thinking. No longer do I believe that prospects purchase **solely on price**. And did my thinking change from distributor thinking all the way to leadership thinking with this one story or real life adventure?

No. That would be too easy, wouldn't it? But you have changed my thinking at least a little bit. You'll have to tell me more stories or give me more examples over the next few weeks to gradually get my thinking all the way to leadership thinking.

So what's another story to change my thinking about price?

How about the "Pizza Story" to reinforce my thinking? It goes like this:

"Big Al, did you ever order pizza? Did you ever feel like just taking it easy and not cooking an evening meal? Did you ever feel like picking up the telephone and ordering a pizza delivered to your home while you watched videos or television?

"Of course you have. Everyone orders pizza on occasion. But is that the most inexpensive way to have a pizza? No way. You are paying for someone else to prepare it and for someone else to deliver it to your home. That's definitely more expensive than growing the ingredients yourself, preparing and cooking the pizza yourself, and definitely more expensive than purchasing a simple frozen pizza and cooking it yourself.

"So why do you spend the extra money? Taste? Better quality? Convenience? Comfort? And you probably spent two or three times as much money by not preparing it yourself!"

Whoops! You got me. Even I don't buy on price alone. And now my thinking edges just a bit closer to leadership thinking.

Just think of all the possibilities of proving to your distributor that people don't buy on the lowest price.

* You could stand outside an expensive shoe store in the shopping mall and watch all the ladies leaving with their purchases.

* You could simply ask women, "Do you buy the cheapest jewelry or the cheapest perfume?"

* Do men buy the cheapest beer in bulk? Or do they pay premium prices at their local bar?

* Or is there one dentist in the city who charges the lowest price? Does he have all the dental business in that city?

* Most airplanes have a first class section. Who sits there?

* Is buying a concert ticket the least expensive way to listen to your favorite music?

Or maybe a simple conversation might do?

One of my distributors still insists that people buy on price. He couldn't understand why someone would pay more for convenience, quality, a relationship with the seller, etc. So here is how the conversation went:

***

Distributor: If we don't have the lowest-priced product, how can you expect me to make any sales?

Big Al: Do you always buy at the lowest price?

Distributor: What do you mean?

Big Al: Let's say that you stop at the gas station to put fuel in your car. Do you ever buy a drink, a candy bar or a snack?

Distributor: Sometimes. Not often though.

Big Al: Does the gas station offer the lowest price of your drink or snack? Or could you have purchased them cheaper in bulk at the local warehouse superstore?

Distributor: Okay, maybe sometimes I shop for convenience, but not often.

Big Al: If you are always shopping for the lowest price, do you constantly go from store to store to compare prices?

Distributor: Well, sometimes I don't have the time, so I guess you're right. Sometimes I might pay more.

Big Al: Do you shop on the Internet for the lowest price?

Distributor: Sometimes. It's a lot of hassle trying to visit all the different websites and figure out what the shipping costs might be. And then I'm not sure if the website with the lowest price is legitimate. And then if I haven't purchased from them before, I have to fill out all my information again in those long forms, and then the new credit card information ... and I think I get the point.

Big Al: If we make it easy, convenient and friendly for our customers, they won't care about the lowest price. Our customers want quality products, at a fair price, and with today's lack of customer service, they enjoy talking to a "live" person.

***

Simple little conversations and stories can change people. Instead of unfocused, random conversations with our potential leaders, we need to be teaching new lessons and viewpoints to help others rise in their business.

Want another example of a conversation with a distributor?

Now, you be the judge. After reading this conversation, ask yourself, "Am I willing to invest time in teaching this person to be a leader?"

Here is the conversation with an unmotivated, broke, and afraid-to-take-personal-responsibility downline distributor (now, that is a hint).

***

Big Al: You should at least invest $100 a month ($25 a week) in your business for products, sales aids, training materials, promotions, advertising, etc. Are you willing to do that?

Distributor: Nope. Can't do that. I don't have any money. Once I pay my bills, there's nothing left. Can't I just collect a few bonus checks first, and then build a business?

Big Al: Life doesn't work that way. Let's look at your present situation. You have worked ten years for the same company. You are an adult. And, you are telling me that you haven't managed to save $100 total in all those years of work? Are you telling me you haven't had the business skill or ability to save a total of $10 a year? That is only one week's work on a paper route or part-time job.

Distributor: Yep. The situation is grim. But, all my money goes to paying bills. If I had a few extra dollars every month, I would invest it in my business, honest!

Big Al: How much do you pay for your enhanced cable television and Internet?

Distributor: About $100 a month. But, I could never give that up. That is our only form of entertainment.

Big Al: Do you ever eat out? Or, do you always cook your meals?

Distributor: We eat dinner out about twice a week. I know it's expensive, but sometimes we're just so-o-o-o tired when we come home from work. That's about $90 a week, about $360 a month, but we do deserve a break now and then. And yes, I buy lunch two or three times a week also, but I consider it a good break from the boredom of the office.

Big Al: Do you smoke or drink?

Distributor: Cigarettes are $10 a pack, and I smoke a pack a day, but hey, I am addicted. I can't do anything about that. You don't expect me to give up smoking to build a business, do you? And don't get on me about my drinking. It is the only way I can unwind after a tough day.

Big Al: What about weekends? Are they free? Could you take on a few odd jobs to have a little extra money to build your business?

Distributor: Yeah, I have weekends off, but I have a lot of chores and duties around the house. It is the only time of the week I can catch up and get a bit of rest, and maybe get in a game of golf.

Big Al: Golf? Do you pay for green fees and clubs and drinks and ...?

Distributor: I'm not putting away my golf clubs to build a business. Golf takes only three or four hours of my week anyway.

Big Al: So what plan do you have to free up $25 a week to build your network marketing business?

Distributor: That's what I'm asking you. Tell me what I can do to get my business going. Nothing has worked so far. So what are you going to do about it, Mr. Sponsor?

***

Sound familiar?

I don't think a lot of commentary is needed.

Even in the poorest neighborhood, you will find people who order pizza and pay extra to have it delivered to their door. People who have expensive mobile phones. People who pay to go to parties and concerts.

It is not a matter of not having money. It is a matter of priorities. If your prospect fails to perceive enough value in your opportunity, there never will be money for promotion, advertising, training and samples.

The solution is obvious. We must create the value of our opportunity in our distributor's minds ... or, make the choice of not investing time with this distributor to teach him to become a leader. Unfortunately for the distributor, most times we have to make the decision to invest our time with someone who is ready.

Can't think of any stories to use for your problems?

Well, why not borrow another explanation that I use?

Let's say that your new potential leader thinks this:

"I can't become successful because my sponsor doesn't help me."

"It is too hard for me to become successful because my sponsor dropped out, only orders products, never calls, and all my upline are useless products users who don't want to build a business. There is no one to help me. I can't do it alone. All the blame lies with my low-life, lazy, good-for-nothing, bonus-collecting sponsor."

Why not tell your potential leader this:

"Do we have any leaders in our company? Of course we do. If it takes a leader to sponsor and develop a leader, that means every leader in your company was sponsored by a leader. What are the odds of that? I don't know. Let's look."

Then systematically go through all the leaders in your company and see who really sponsored them into the business. I bet you will both be surprised that most leaders were sponsored by somebody who didn't care, somebody who quit or just dropped out.

Think about it. Pick all the networking leaders you know. Some leaders have successful upline sponsors – and most leaders were sponsored by **unsuccessful** distributors.

Many of the top networking leaders today had upline sponsors who were total jerks or even dropped out of the business. They made their success from their **own** efforts, not from handouts and special gifts and favors.

Or look at it this way.

Most upline sponsors have some successful distributors **and** some unsuccessful distributors.

If both unsuccessful and successful distributors have the same sponsor, what is the only variable?

That's right, the distributor.

This conversation tells it all.

Some years ago, I had this telephone conversation with a disgruntled distributor. He couldn't figure out why he and his distributors were unlucky, yet other distributors were lucky and quickly became leaders.

This distributor hated his company, his products, his upline, his downline, and network marketing in general. The conversation went something like this:

***

Distributor: I can't become successful in network marketing because my company is destroying my business. They ship products late. Bonus checks are wrong. The staff is rude when my downline calls for help. They have too many back orders.

Big Al: Are there any successful leaders in your network marketing company?

Distributor: Yes.

Big Al: Do these leaders get their products and bonus checks late, and suffer from backorders also?

Distributor: Well, yes. But it's different for them.

Big Al: Do you think that the home office personnel are only rude to your downline, or do you think the successful network marketing leaders in your company have downlines who talk to the same employees?

Distributor: Okay, okay. I get your point. I guess the company, its products, and its employees are not responsible for my success or **lack of success**. In fact, no matter what they do they can't just make me successful. So, if other leaders are successful with my company, I guess it is not the company that caused me to fail.

Big Al: That's right. A company can't make you successful.

Distributor: I guess the real problem is that my network marketing company is not going through the momentum phase. All the successful leaders have an organization already. I can't build a big organization now because the company isn't growing.

Big Al: When a company is growing fast, is it possible to have a particular group growing slowly, or even getting smaller?

Distributor: I guess so. Sure, I can see where a group with a lousy leader could be disintegrating while the overall company is growing.

Big Al: When the company is growing slowly, or not at all, is it possible to have a particular group growing fast?

Distributor: Uh, yes. I guess a leader could build a fantastic organization while the rest of the distributors in the company are sitting on their backsides. So, the fact that my company is not in the momentum stage really doesn't explain why my business is going poorly.

Now, after thinking about it, I see that the **real problem** with my business is that I have a useless, lazy, greedy, worthless sponsor. He never calls me, has bad breath, doesn't know anything about our business, shows too much hype, sometimes is too boring, and really hasn't done a thing to build my business!

Big Al: Tell me a little bit about your sponsor. Does he have other first-level distributors? How are they doing?

Distributor: Well, my sponsor has about 15 first-level distributors. Most have dropped out. Some are struggling like me. And, three or four are doing pretty good.

Big Al: The three or four distributors who are doing pretty good ... who is their sponsor?

Distributor: Ouch! I see. The successful distributors have the exact same sponsor as I do. You're right. I guess my problem isn't my sponsor.

Big Al: Maybe you should stop looking for a better company, a better time to join another company, and a better sponsor. Sounds like these aren't your problem. Do you know what your problem is?

Distributor: It must be something else. I just can't put my finger on it. I know that somebody is keeping me from success, somebody close by. **I just don't know who.** I will let you know when I figure it out.

***

I get a lot of phone calls like this. These distributors never ask for advice, so I don't give any advice. It just isn't their time yet to move towards becoming a leader.

Unsuccessful distributors are always looking for **someone else** to make them successful. They believe that success comes from **outside** influences such as the company or their sponsor. **Outside** influences can't make anyone successful or unsuccessful.

The real, ugly, disgusting secret in network marketing is that success comes from **within** the network marketing distributor. It is a personal thing.

Don't give up control.

If you give up control and the responsibility for your success to your upline sponsor, you simultaneously allow your upline to **control your failure**. No one purposely goes into network marketing saying:

"I hope my upline sponsor decides to make me a success and not a failure. I hope my upline is in a good mood today."

To give up control of our networking future so easily sounds ridiculous, doesn't it?

Ask successful networking leaders and they will tell you they are **self-made** successes. Most people find it easy to take credit for their success.

But if this logic holds true, then every unsuccessful networking distributor would be a self-made failure. Gee, you never hear the **self-made failure** explanation used in conversation.

This line of thinking reminds me of the old saying:

"Behind every successful man is a woman."

Of course, behind every **unsuccessful** man is **also** a woman, but no one ever brings that up (with the exception of every drunk feeling sorry for himself at the local tavern on Friday night).

This is getting easy.

Yes, teaching your potential leaders new ways of thinking is easy. The hard part was knowing **what** to teach and **how** to teach it. But now you have the formula.

You simply take a problem, and then figure out what distributor thinking is and what leadership thinking is for that problem. Then give them concrete examples and stories to gradually move your potential leader's thinking from distributor thinking to leadership thinking. Your potential leaders will **believe** their own conclusions.

You then end up with a person who **thinks like a leader** and is on the path to **becoming a leader**. This is a measurable, proven, efficient track to follow instead of just randomly saying, "I will build a relationship and hope this friendly distributor magically becomes a leader."

Building leaders is easy once you teach them how to handle problems.

If you master this principle of leadership, then you will have less stress, more time, less rejection, no doom and gloom days, no politics, fewer challenges ... and it will be lot more fun living life as a leader.

If your leaders don't master this principle, then you will hear this very unpleasant conversation from them:

"The customer hated the product, the home office didn't make a timely refund, so I lost my distributor. It looks like the company is ruining my business. I want to move to another company where they don't have problems."

You and I don't want to hear that conversation, so let's fix that now.

It's weird, but no one ever thinks about it.

Several years ago, I returned from England where the network marketing community has an **unusual** and **outrageous** perspective.

I thought they were absolutely crazy, but ... I noticed that the network marketing community in the United States has the **exact same distorted** perspective. Is this a secret insanity virus spreading worldwide?

Networkers everywhere are killing their businesses. And they don't understand why. Imagine investing hundreds or even thousands of hours into your business, and then systematically destroying your business with an **incorrect point of view.**

First, a little background.

How many hours do you think the average networking leader spends doing the following tasks?

* Listening to downline personal problems.

* Listening to downline business problems.

* Making numerous telephone calls to the home office following up lost shipments or product shortages.

* Apologizing for incorrect statements made by the upline leaders or home office staff.

* Playing referee between jealous distributors fighting over a single enrollment.

* Berating home office staff who don't understand network marketing.

* Keeping track of all the telephone calls that weren't returned promptly.

* Worrying about greed destroying certain members of the organization.

* Groaning about unfair treatment and lack of recognition.

* Trying to recover business that was stolen by unfair competition.

* Discussing the company's lack of leadership and responsiveness with other disgruntled sales leaders.

If you add up the hours, it's a 40-hour week!

These activities take **time**. How much time can a leader afford on these non-productive, non-revenue-generating activities?

These activities take **physical effort**. Leaders are physically exhausted after marathon telephone conversations with professional victims complaining that the world is against them.

These activities take **mental effort**. Leaders lose their mental energy fighting these losing battles. After one of these battles, the leader prefers to become comatose and watch television. There is no enthusiasm left for a prospecting campaign.

Who has the problem?

Guess what? The distributor doesn't have the real problem here. **The leaders have the problem!**

The leaders have an incorrect viewpoint. Here is what the **unsuccessful** leaders believe:

In order to be successful in network marketing:

* 100% of the home office employees must be perfect.

* 100% of all distributors must be honorable, charitable, problem-free citizens without a hint of greed.

* 100% of all distributors must never quit.

* 100% of all telephone calls must be answered the way they want them.

* 100% of the home office staff should become instantly available when they call.

* 100% of all upline leaders should be perfect role models who never make a mistake while speaking.

* Distributors are never selfish.

* 100% of all decisions must be perfect.

* 100% of all decisions must work out perfectly in the future.

Everything must be perfect, or they'll just complain and destroy their business, and then look for a new venture with the perfect leaders, the perfect home office staff, the perfect compensation plan, the perfect product at the perfect price that satisfies 100% of all people 100% of the time, etc., etc., etc.

Yuck! As Zig Ziglar would say, **"That's some stinking thinking!"**

So, unsuccessful leaders quickly sink into "fix-it" mode and spend the rest of their mediocre careers making sure nothing bad ever happens to anyone in their downline, upline, or company. Now, that's going to be pretty hard in this world. Providing a protective bubble around every distributor is not only impossible, it is insane.

This is what unsuccessful leaders say regularly:

"It's a crisis! It's a crisis! Should I fix it now?"

No.

If your business can't survive a crisis or two, maybe it's time to go back and build a better foundation. And, there will be lots of problems in your future no matter how well you build your foundation because ...

People are human!

That's right. Your company, your upline, and even your downline are human. And as humans, they have certain characteristics, such as:

* Humans make mistakes. Only computers are perfect, and computers don't want to be distributors.

* Humans are often selfish.

* Humans are professional quitters. They quit school, quit jobs, quit marriages, quit diets, quit New Year's resolutions, and quit network marketing programs.

* Humans often fail to return telephone calls.

* Humans are often rude.

* Humans take people for granted. They don't show appreciation to their upline or downline when appropriate.

* Humans love to criticize. It makes them feel superior and helps them to forget their own personal problems.

* Humans make terrible decisions. Why do you think there are so many divorces? Or why do you think so many people lose at the horse races? Or why do we eat too many donuts?

* Humans think they are always right. After all, who do you know that deliberately goes out of his way to be totally wrong?

So when distributors, upline or home office personnel make mistakes, are rude, criticize, or quit ... don't be surprised!

They are just being human!

Why fight human nature?

Why not just accept people as they are?

As humans.

This is the point of view that **successful** leaders take. They don't waste time trying to change people, fix their perceived problems, or trying to eliminate all the problems in the world.

Successful leaders learn to **manage** problems, not fix problems.

There is a difference.

Imagine that you could work hard and magically fix all the problems with your downline, upline, and network marketing company. Whew! That was hard.

Now, since you fixed all the problems today, what are the chances that there will be some new problems tomorrow?

100%!!!

Yes, more problems tomorrow, the day after tomorrow, and every day in the future. There will always be problems.

Successful leaders accept this fact. They simply learn to **live with the problems** instead of stressing over each problem for the rest of their lives.

Look at it this way.

There is no such thing as a perfect network marketing company. All the companies hire humans! So, of course there are lots of mistakes and problems.

What do unsuccessful distributors do? If they see that their present network marketing company has a problem, they quit! They join another network marketing company and hope they never have a problem.

What kind of crazy thinking is that?

All network marketing companies have problems.

Successful distributors and leaders realize that:

All network marketing companies have problems. You simply choose the company that you wish to have your problems with.

Then, get over it. Accept the problems and get on with business.

Women understand this principle, "All network marketing companies have problems, you simply choose the company that you wish to have your problems with." Why?

Because they know that:

"All men have problems. You simply choose the man you wish to have your problems with."

Men, of course, don't understand this. Because women are perfect, we can't see the analogy.

Let your competitors try to fix the problems, fix human nature, and jump from one company to another. Encourage your competitors to do it.

Why?

This will keep your competitors busy while you build a large and successful networking business. You'll have exclusive access to all the best prospects because your competitors are too busy trying to fix problems!

But don't I have to fix some of the problems?

No.

Our businesses will be quite successful if we just concentrate on **developing three or four leaders**. Once we have three or four trained people who think like we do ... **we're invincible!**

Developing leaders is **everything** in our business. Distributors may come and go, problems may come and go, problems may come and stay, but if we develop long-term, loyal leaders, we will be here forever with regular bonus checks.

All these other problems don't have anything to do with **locating, training and developing our three or four good leaders.**

Let's look at a typical crisis #1.

Your distributor received his order of 20 different products and one product was missing. The missing item was Donut Blend #2.

Your distributor calls his sponsor and says:

"Help! Help! My order is incomplete. I don't know how many items are missing, but it's all wrong. Do you think the company is going out of business?"

It is a **natural** human tendency to **exaggerate** slightly when describing a personal problem.

The sponsor accepts the problem and becomes depressed. He worries about what would happen if his distributor quits over this massive product shortage.

So, the sponsor calls his sponsor and says:

"Help! Help! The company has stopped shipping products and is taking our distributors' money! Why are they attacking and destroying our business?"

It's a **natural** human tendency to **exaggerate** slightly when describing a personal problem.

His sponsor panics over this massive, career-destroying problem. So he calls his sponsor (that's you) and says:

"Help! Help! The company stopped shipping products and sent a SWAT team out and is now shooting our distributors! You have to stop the killings!"

Like I mentioned, it's a **natural** human tendency to **exaggerate** slightly when describing a personal problem.

So, by the time you have received the problem, it is a big, big problem.

How are you going to react?

Are you going to call the home office and add a little exaggeration to the story? Not if you're a successful leader.

As a successful leader you have a rock-solid, stable viewpoint. You know that the **only thing that counts** is that you **locate and develop three or four good leaders** - period.

All other problems are just a distraction that you can ignore.

What do you do? You reply to your panic-stricken leader and say:

"Missing products, eh? Well, I don't have access to the home office shipping computer, so why not email them the details, send a copy to me, and they will take care of it."

Boom! You are done. That's it. No more hysteria or involvement.

Now this relatively minor problem is **manageable**. The distributor with the problem must write down the details in an email. That's good. Why?

* Writing down the details is hard. Most people would rather pass the problem on to their upline rather than handle it themselves. After all, it is just human nature. Why not make a simple exaggerated telephone call? That is easier than producing a written report.

* Writing down the details usually limits the amount of exaggeration.

* Most people will check their facts again before committing themselves in writing.

So, what happens?

The distributor checks the shipping box again and magically finds the missing product, Donut Blend #2.

Problem managed. You are moving on with your business of **locating and developing three or four good leaders** for your business.

In all of my years of network marketing, only one person ever wrote down all the facts and sent those facts to the company and me. One. That's it.

And here is what happened when I received his fax with his problems. I went to lunch. I told myself I would deal with the problem-laced fax in the morning.

The next morning I got a call from this distributor thanking me for taking care of his problem. It seems the home office called him back, sorted everything out, and he was satisfied.

Well, I simply placed that fax in the trash. I never read it, and I never really knew what the problems were. All I know is that I have saved hours, days and weeks of time trying to fix problems.

"Hey! That's a pretty good perspective on how this networking business really works."

What would happen if your downline adopted this point of view?

Massive growth. Massive sales. Massive bonus checks.

Wouldn't it be nice if your downline never complained? Instead, they simply accepted problems as part of life and then went on their way to build their business?

Well, that would be a perfect world. However, there is no rule that says we can't educate and train our downlines towards this goal.

Can you imagine how powerful your opportunity meetings would be if everyone was positive and focused on their goal of locating and developing **three or four good leaders?** The atmosphere would be magic! With so much positive energy in the room, guests would join without even hearing a presentation! Prospects want to be involved with positive people who know where they are going.

What about other problems?

* Can a human make a mistake during a business presentation?

* Can there be a typographical error in a brochure?

* Can an underpaid newspaper reporter jealously write an unfair story about your company or your products?

* Can an upline leader tell lies, steal customers, counterfeit distributor applications and steal your dog?

Yes! It happens.

So what!

All these type of problems have nothing to do with your ultimate focused goal of **locating and developing your three or four leaders.** (Notice a common theme here yet?)

Let's look at crisis #2.

Back to England. Several years ago, I gave an opportunity meeting presentation to about 50 people. It was in a small hotel room in the north of England.

In the back of the room was a brand new distributor. She brought along her husband and her 11-month old daughter.

Also in the back of the room was a prospect with a $1,000 pin stripe suit, manicured nails, the perfect tan, a replica of a very expensive watch, and ... an attitude. He looked like the stereotypical New York City stockbroker.

What do you do when the baby cries?

As I proceeded with my presentation, occasionally the baby made a bit of noise. Okay, the baby cried. It wasn't really loud, but it was distracting.

Now, here is the question:

Does a baby crying have anything to do with **locating and developing your three or four good leaders?** (Notice a common theme here yet?)

No!

A crying baby is not a problem. It is a non-event. It is totally manageable by simply ignoring the crying and continuing with the opportunity meeting.

So I did.

Guess what happened when the meeting was over?

The well-dressed guest left! He was completely turned off by the baby's crying.

His parting remarks?

"How could any professional business allow a crying baby to interfere or distract prospects during a business presentation? I couldn't possibly join a non-professional organization like that!"

Now here is the million-dollar question you have to ask yourself as a business-builder and networking leader:

"If my prospect quits or doesn't even join because an 11-month old baby cries, will this prospect ever be one of my **three or four good leaders?**"

The obvious answer is "No."

At best, this prospect might become a "temporary" distributor. He will quit at the first sign of distress, problems, hurt feelings, or stress. Or, what if his guest doesn't show up at the next meeting? This person would be devastated!

So whether or not this "temporary" distributor joins or not, it would not make any difference in one's long-term networking career. There will be plenty of bigger obstacles in this person's career that will cause him to quit.

Look at it this way. This prospect quit before he even started.

Why?

Because he heard the crying of an 11-month old baby who didn't even recognize his existence. The 11-month old baby **didn't even know or care that this prospect existed!**

Yet, this 11-month old baby **had the power and control to make decisions** for this weak-willed, well-dressed prospect.

If this so-called prospect is going to let 11-month old babies make decisions for him, how well is he going to do in his own business? Not well.

Should you fix the problem?

No.

It would be a total waste of time.

Let's say that you banned babies from the opportunity meeting. Maybe you hired babysitters or told families they weren't welcomed if they had children. Anyway, you fix the problem of babies crying at opportunity meetings.

So what?

* What if the meeting room was too hot? Wouldn't this picky, weak-willed prospect still refuse to join?

* What if the meeting next door made too much noise?

* What if the speaker made a mistake during the presentation?

* What if someone had a bad cough?

See the problem?

The problem is with the prospect, not with the circumstances around the prospect.

You can't go through life, walking in front of this prospect, and say:

* "Please smile when you walk past my prospect."

* "Please don't say anything bad about our company in front of my prospect."

* "Please don't let it rain while my prospect is coming to our meeting."

This prospect believes that circumstances must be right in order for him to become successful. In other words, he is saying **that success is outside of himself.**

He is dependent on circumstances to make him successful. And he hopes that the 11-month old baby doesn't make any more decisions for him.

Is this prospect ever going to develop into one of your **three or four good leaders?**

No. The 11-month old baby might have a better chance.

Leadership has nothing to do with the clothes you wear.

Who would you rather have in your organization?

1. The mother who brought her 11-month old baby and her husband to the opportunity meeting, or

2. The well-dressed, weak-willed prospect who takes directions and career decisions from an 11-month old baby?

The answer is obvious, once you understand the principle of **locating and developing three or four good leaders.** Leaders are everything. They are your long-term security.

They are your keys to solid growth and consistent bonus checks.

Almost everything else you do in networking marketing is trivial.

Your major effort is to concentrate on **locating and developing three or four good leaders.**

Most of the other things we do are a waste of time. Want some examples?

Discussing company politics, arguing with know-it-all distributors, re-training uplines, arranging chairs at opportunity meetings, re-writing the prospecting brochure for the thirty-first time, arranging product displays, memorizing sales pitches, holding hands with weak-willed prospects, correcting people when they are wrong, scolding distributors for missing meetings, wishing you got more money for your efforts, demanding immediate shipment of backorders, demanding that everyone in every circumstance was treated fairly, listening to petty grievances, giving pity to people with hurt egos, trying to save professional victims, forcing distributors to go to trainings they don't want to attend, trying to find somebody to blame, wishing people had the same vision you have, telling management how to do their job, etc., etc., etc.

We don't become successful leaders by solving these problems. And, we don't become successful leaders by sponsoring and replacing "temporary" distributors.

Even the President and the Pope can't solve all the problems.

Think about the resources they have. Money? Staff? They are famous. And yet, even they can't solve every problem. So what about us with even fewer resources? Of course we can't solve all the problems, so let's get over it.

We become successful leaders by **locating and developing three or four other good leaders.**

"Network Marketing Crisis Center, may I help you?"

Make sure this is not how you answer your telephone. Instead, educate and train your new distributors and potential leaders that problems are natural. Problems are part of life and will be here tomorrow and every day of our lives.

So instead of fixing, stressing over, and worrying about problems, simply manage problems and get on with life. You'll have more free time, less stress, and the lifestyle to enjoy those big, big bonus checks.

And, you'll find yourself easily answering questions and handling problems when you are focused on locating and developing **three or four good leaders.**

For instance, if you live 40 miles from your company's home office, you will have distributors ask you:

"Why don't you go over and visit the home office more often?"

You can answer:

"Because visiting the home office has nothing to do with **locating and developing my three or four good leaders.**"

Or distributors will ask,

"Why can't we have Donut Blend #8 in chocolate?"

You can answer:

"What does that have to do with **locating and developing our three or four good leaders?**"

Or distributors will say,

"Mary spoke too long during the opportunity meeting."

You can answer:

"What does that have to do with **locating and developing our three or four good leaders?"**

See? It's easy.

Once we understand the principles and have the proper perspective on our networking business - **everything gets easier!**

And finally, in case you didn't notice the principle yet, here it is:

Our job as leaders is to simply locate and develop three or four good leaders.

The rest of our activities are simply "non-events." They just don't matter.

Choosing how to handle time-wasting problems.

Maybe you've had this happen: your distributor calls and says:

"The product is too expensive, the compensation plan doesn't pay enough, the management stinks ... and you are a worthless sponsor!"

Don't you just hate telephone conversations with your distributors when they are having a bad attitude day?

Nothing is right with you or the company. Everything is broken and your distributor has **100 reasons** why everything is impossible to fix. And even if your distributor died and went to heaven on his bad attitude day, he would just complain about altitude sickness.

So what can you do?

Nothing.

The problem is **not** with the problems. You can argue with your distributor that everything is fine, can be fixed, will be improved, and things will just keep getting better and better. No matter how persuasive your argument, you will lose.

Even if you personally solve all the current problems, your distributor will locate or create new problems. You are in a lose-lose situation.

For instance, your distributor telephones and says:

"I called the home office and I couldn't get through."

Well, what can we do?

We can solve the problem for our distributor. We can pick him up, put him in our car, drive him to the home office, walk him inside, cut up the phone lines and say:

"Now talk to my distributor!"

We solved the problem, didn't we? But as soon as that problem is solved, then what? Our distributor has another problem.

"Well, I got my products in the box, and I cut my finger opening the box."

Okay. We run an ad in the local newspaper and we hire someone to help our new distributor. The new help comes and his only job in life is to open our distributor's boxes so he doesn't cut his fingers.

Well, the next problem our new distributor has is:

"My sponsor is a jerk!"

Instead of taking it personally, you offer:

"Why don't you get a different sponsor other than me?"

Do you realize some people have problems all their lives? And they are going to have to live with these problems. You can't solve all their problems.

You can spend all your time and all your effort trying to solve problems and make things perfect, and you are never going to get even close to getting started, are you?

And remember, the President, the Pope, and even the Queen of England have tremendous resources at their disposal. And even with all of these resources, they can't solve all of their problems.

We have limited resources. We don't have a chance.

Well, if you can't fix the problems, what can you do?

As I said before, the problem is not with the problems. The real problem is **inside** your distributor's mind. Your distributor has made a **decision** that success is **not within himself.**

Your distributor has decided to believe that success is **outside of his control** and can only be found in outside circumstances. In other words, he doesn't believe he can become successful because success can only be achieved in a perfect world, with perfect people, with perfect products, with perfect prices, with perfect compensation plans, with ... well, you get the picture.

Our world is full of problems. They just won't go away - ever. So, success must be achieved in spite of these constant problems.

To decide or not to decide.
That is the question.

Leaders understand success. It is like someone gave us an operator's manual. We realize that in every situation, some people are successful, and some are not. So success can't be dependent on the situation. Success must be dependent on the person.

Then why do some people become successful and others do not - in the **same** circumstances or situations?

The answer lies in the six inches (15 cm) between our ears. It's how we **decide** to think.

Yes, the key word here is "decide."

This is a personal decision about what we think. There is no mind control from devious villains. There are no laws that restrict us from deciding how we wish to think. Each of us has the power to decide how we wish to think in any given situation.

This simple decision is what determines our success. I will give you an easy demonstration.

Wow! I am here!

At a recent training session, I spoke about the decisions we make inside of our mind. My conversation with the group went something like this:

Me: Were there any problems getting here today?

Group: We had to take off work. It is a weekday. That was a big problem.

Me: Did that problem keep many of your distributors from coming today?

Group: Yes. They **decided** that they couldn't take off work.

Me: Yet, you **decided** to come, right?

Group: We **decided** to come and miss a day at our jobs.

Me: Was there bad traffic coming to this meeting?

Group: Yes. Terrible traffic.

Me: Any other problems coming today?

Group: It is raining. Maybe even flooding in some areas. But we **decided** to come anyway.

Me: Any other problems?

Group: Some of our friends said we are crazy and having your own business never works. We **decided** to ignore them and come anyway.

Me: What about parking? There is no convenient parking around here.

Group: We had to park several blocks away and walk in the rain. However, we came so far that we **decided** not to turn back. We just got a little wet coming here.

Me: So you came here today even though all those problems **never got solved**, right?

Group: We are here. The problems are still there. I guess our distributors decided that all those problems had to go away before they could come to this training and become successful. You know what? There's always going to be bad weather, long distances to drive, bad parking, inconvenient days, and ... **yikes!** Our distributors will never become successful if they believe that problems have to go away!!!

Me: What if your distributors quit and joined another company?

Group: Even if they joined another company, there will still be bad weather, long distances to drive, bad parking, inconvenient days ... hey! Switching companies doesn't solve anything. You are just going to experience the **same problems** with another company.

Me: So what can you do to help your distributors? You can't solve all the problems.

Group: The only thing we can do is to teach our new distributors that they have the power in their own minds to make decisions. They can look at the problem and choose to decide which group they want to be in: the group that **decides** that the problem is **larger** than their dream for success, or the group that **decides** that their dream for success is **larger** than the problem.

So why do unsuccessful distributors complain, fail, and quit?

Because their sponsor never told them the truth about problems. Most distributors believe that problems must be solved. They never look around and notice that the leaders in their group experience the **exact same problems**, yet the leaders are successful.

They don't understand that problems exist. Most times we can't fix the problem. However, we can decide to choose how we react to the problem.

I think our job is to educate our new distributors that all of their problems really occur in the six inches between their ears. Then our new distributors will recognize this phenomenon when they hear themselves say, "**In my mind the real problem is ...** "

Who's on this cruise ship?

For 25 years, I have organized the MLM Cruise. Networkers from around the world come to spend seven days relaxing and learning from each other. Let me give you a few problems and reasons why these network marketers shouldn't be there:

* We have to take one week off work.

* We had to save up money for airfare.

* We had to save up money for the cruise.

* We couldn't find a babysitter.

* It is an important time at work.

* We get seasick.

* It is too far.

* No one offered to pay my way.

* We have never done this before.

* What will the neighbors think?

* We have to pay port taxes, too!

* The cabins are too small.

* There won't be anything to do.

* We won't know anybody.

And yet, despite all these problems (and I should add that none of these problems were solved), every year network marketers still **decide** to go on this cruise.

Going on this cruise has **nothing** to do with the problems. It has everything to do with deciding to go.

Yet there are thousands of networkers who "wanted" to go on this cruise, but decided that they could not go - because there were problems.

Are there problems and reasons why your business won't work?

Sure there are. Lots of problems and reasons that make it impossible to succeed, right?

Wrong.

The problems have nothing to do with success. The problems are outside of us and we can personally **decide** what we think.

We can think:

"Sure there are problems. Most of these problems are with us every day. Yet, other leaders succeed in spite of these problems. Maybe I will **decide** to become successful, too."

Or we can think:

"Sure there are problems. That is why I can't become successful. Poor me. I wish Mom would fix everything for me. The world has put up barriers to my success. These problems are much bigger than my desire to succeed. I am a professional victim. I guess I will **decide** to fail."

Do we really think like this?

Yes.

Kind of pathetic, isn't it? I think we all should keep our spouse or friends close by so they can point out and remind us when we **decide** to accept "failure thinking." Hmmm, some people will eagerly volunteer for this assignment.

So let's look at some of the problems in our network marketing businesses. Let's see if these problems really are bigger than our dreams for success.

Problems.

* The products are too expensive.

* The shipping costs too much.

* My sponsor doesn't help me.

* I wish my sponsor didn't help me.

* They didn't mention my name in the newsletter.

* The orders arrive late.

* Mistakes in my downline report.

* The bonus check was for the wrong amount.

* Nobody listens to me.

* The company doesn't care about my problems.

* The meetings are too far away.

* The compensation plan pays too little.

* Our competitors have no problems (we are really feeling sorry for ourselves here!)

* We should get a salary.

* We should be paid on effort, not results.

* My downline works hard but gets discouraged.

* There isn't enough retail profit.

* We don't have a good video to show prospects.

* The president won't talk to me.

* Nobody is making any money.

* Nobody is making any sales.

* Nobody is recruiting.

* The volume requirements are too high.

* The volume requirements are too low.

* We should get paid twice a day.

* The distributor kit is too hard to read.

* The company insists on training to get ahead.

* The company offers no training.

* The company should change the compensation plan.

* The company makes too many changes.

* My downline never calls me.

* No one wants to join.

* The new person doesn't make enough.

* The leaders don't make enough.

* We should get a "signing bonus" when we start.

* My community is too conservative.

* My spouse doesn't understand me.

* My children don't listen to me.

* My job takes too much time.

* Saturdays are for football.

* The company makes too many mistakes.

* My distributors will all probably join the next new company.

* I am perfect and the rest of the world disagrees.

* The order form is difficult to fill out.

* It's too hard.

And despite all of these problems, the leaders in our company are still successful!!!

And the leaders have the exact same problems we do.

Why all this emphasis on handling problems?

Because problems happen. They will continue to happen. And you can't rescue your potential leader every time he says:

"Oh no, now we have a problem.
And it is a huge big problem.
I feel the disaster approaching."

At least one bad event will happen to your business this year. That's life. It is no big deal.

No business can go on forever with lucky events followed by good fortune, followed by miraculous good news.

We either teach our new potential leader to handle problems … or, we won't have a new leader on our team.

I don't know anyone who joined the perfect business, at the perfect time, with the perfect product, with the perfect pricing, in the perfect market, with the perfect compensation plan, with the perfect sponsor and the perfect downline.

Do you?

We all want our business to have good fortune forever, but occasionally someone steps on our dreams.

And for some of us, people step on our dreams more often.

If you can't think of any problems in your networking business, see if these look familiar:

* Your company backorders or discontinues your group's favorite product.

* The local trash tabloid reports that your company's president is secretly a two-headed alien who performs secret animal sacrifices.

* Your disgruntled downline distributors form their own competing company and try to steal your leaders.

* Or, out of thousands of product orders, your company made a mistake on someone's order (shudder, stress, check our wills, sound the panic alert!)

So what happens when your business has the occasional but inevitable problems?

Do you lose your leaders?

Do you spend hours on the phone trying to salvage your downline?

Do you apologize, sympathize, and worry into the night?

I hope not.

You should prepare yourself in **advance** for problems. Your company will have problems, your upline will have problems, your downline will have problems, and that's just how life is. If you don't believe that problems will ever happen to your business, trust me, that illusion will pass shortly.

How do you prepare your leaders for bad news, backorders, fulfillment mistakes, jealous politics, hurt feelings, phone calls mixed up or not returned, etc.?

Simple.

Tell them the truth **in advance**.

You might say something like this:

"John, before you make a total commitment to building your business, you need to know the **facts**.

"Our company is **not perfect**. There will be some problems in the future. Even worse, our company employs **humans**, and you know how they can make mistakes. The good news is that our company tries its best to fix mistakes when they happen. Now that you know there will be problems in the future, **are you still willing to make a total commitment** to build your downline?"

Normally, John will answer,

"No problem. I understand there will be ups and downs. Thanks for being honest with me. There are problems in every job and business, so I know better than to try to look for perfection."

Now, when the inevitable problems do occur, you have prepared your leaders for a little pep talk. Let's say that the problem of the month was ...

The company changed its labels from light green to dark green.

Oooo-hhhh.

Now your downline is really worried.

Your leaders are thinking of switching to another company that offers labels in a very light green. They swear they never want to live through another label color change. Their customers complain. Their distributors feel confused. This problem is now a major crisis and threatens the motivation and belief of your entire downline.

But, you had the **foresight** to prepare your downline for the eventual problems. Here's your pep talk:

"John, remember when you first made the commitment to build your business? We discussed that problems would be in our future and would give us a few stumbling blocks along the way.

"Well, this label color change is one of those problems. It looks like a big deal now, but if we compare it to a ten- or twenty-year career, it is just one of those problems that happens. Sometimes we leap forward, sometimes we take a step or two back, but overall, as leaders, we focus on long-term, steady progress.

"That is what makes us different from the average distributor who has **one** bad experience and quits. Then, the average distributor has to go out and invest and build a brand-new group with a new company. That is a lot of time and money invested in training and building a new business. There is no income coming in, just expenses during these transition periods.

"And just when the average distributor gets to profit in his new network marketing company, B-A-N-G! Another problem pops up. I guess that sums up the difference between average networkers and leaders like us, John. They never make any money because they don't have our long-term vision.

"I bet if their mother served one bad meal, they would never visit her again. If their bank made a mistake on their checking account, they would give up using money. I sure hope you and I can get through to most of your downline that this is just one of those problems along the way. Sure hope that they will have the good business sense we do to see the big picture."

Will your pep talk work?

Not always.

But it is better than no pep talk at all. And, your pep talks always work better when you prepare your leaders early in their careers that no company is perfect and that they should expect problems along the way.

Will you save the distributors in your leaders' downlines?

Not all of them.

Many new networkers believe that success comes from signing an application in a hot new company that will **never** have any problems. They don't believe that network marketing success requires work, effort, patience and long-term commitment. It almost makes you ill to listen to a new distributor say:

"I'm not having anything to do with network marketing. I worked hard for two weeks with an opportunity, and then they had problems. That just ruined any chance I had for success in my life."

I wonder if his job only requires two weeks of effort and then he can retire for life?

So, if a distributor is looking for an excuse not to work — then any excuse will do.

I have never seen a plaque that read:

All the world loves a quitter.

And you can apply this problem principle to new distributors that you personally sponsor also. If you have a slight teasing sense of humor, you could say this when you sponsor an ordinary, beginning distributor. Just as he hands you the signed application and money to join, say this;

"Oh, I forgot to tell you something. Next week our company is going to have a problem, a big problem for our business."

The new distributor clutches his chest and says, "What? A big problem? What is the big problem next week?"

You reply, "Oh, I don't know. Every week there is a problem in business. I just wanted to let you know that there is no perfect business ever. Having problems are just part of any business."

And then, next week when a problem does happen, you can say to your new distributor, "See, I told you there would be a problem."

So what is the difference?

The leaders **choose** to think:

"I choose to become successful in this business. Even if I solve all of these problems, there will be more. I will just get on with building my business."

If it is just that easy, then why don't we all think successfully?

Most times there is a bigger problem at stake. A problem bigger than all of the problems I have listed here. What is that problem? Self-image.

So enough about problems, and as we finish up Volume One on leadership, let's start learning how to develop some personal growth and confidence in our potential leaders to increase their self-image.

Our self-image.

There will never be enough pages in this book to adequately cover the subject of our self-image. I will leave that discussion to the professional psychologists.

However, let's have a limited look at self-image as it applies to how we think.

First, it is easy for us to agree that everyone, including us, has a self-image. It's how we look at ourselves. It is how we view our self-worth. It's our way of describing ourselves to ourselves.

Second, it is **not** easy for us to honestly look at our self-image and what it is doing to our lives.

Third, our self-image will always keep us from becoming more successful than we see ourselves. **It will turn problems and reasons for failure into undeniable truths in our minds.** Our self-image will keep us at the level of success or failure that we are most comfortable with.

Really? Will our self-image keep us from success?

Yes.

So let's take a brief look at this self-image we have of ourselves, and how it tells our mind what to think.

If we **see** ourselves as **total losers**, do you think our prospects and distributors will sense that in our voice and actions? Yes.

Have you ever met someone with a poor self-image? Even if they give the perfect recruiting presentation, their self-image will add this to the end of their presentation:

"And you are probably not interested. Nobody really wants to join. Everyone I have talked to turned me down. The economy is getting bad. Sometimes it rains hard around here. The company doesn't pay enough. My sponsor doesn't help me. It seems that I always pick the wrong deal. I don't know why I'm doing this ..."

If we **see** ourselves as **total winners**, do you think our prospects and distributors will sense that in our voice and actions? Yes.

Now our prospects and distributors will want to be associated with us. They feel we have skills, information, and direction in our lives. They want to follow us to success.

Do some distributors really see themselves as losers and failures?

Yes.

Look around you for proof. Listen to people as they say:

* "Oh, that always happens to me."

* "Oh, I never win at those things."

* "Nobody will ever want to do that."

* "I am sure I can't do that."

* "Only other people can be that fortunate."

* "Nobody loves me."

* "It's too hard."

* "I can't be successful because ..."

* "It is impossible to get ahead because ..."

* "No one will want to join because ..."

All of these statements are coming from these distributors' **minds**. And their minds are being **controlled** by their self-image.

* They see themselves as unsuccessful.

* They see themselves as victims.

* They see themselves as having continuous problems and limitations in their lives.

Some people define themselves and define their lives as victims of problems. If you take away their problems, they wouldn't know who they are!

We all need to ask ourselves:

"How do I see myself? As a victim of problems? Or as a master of my own destiny? Is my success dependent on other people? Outside decisions by others? The weather? The compensation plan? The newsletter?"

How we see ourselves determines how we think, and the **decisions** we make.

Need more proof that self-images control our minds, and the decisions we make?

Have you ever heard of someone on social welfare who wins a million dollars in the lottery? What often happens in a few years?

That person is broke.

That person had a self-image of a social welfare recipient. That person consistently made **decisions** to spend the money unwisely (jewelry, cars, concert tickets, expensive meals, stereos, vacation trips, designer clothes, and horse racing) so that he would return to social welfare, where he felt comfortable.

If this person had a self-image of a rich, successful investor, he would have **decided** to invest in stocks, real estate, or other assets.

Have you ever heard of someone who was a millionaire but lost his fortune? What often happens in a few years?

That person is again a millionaire.

That person had a self-image of being a millionaire. That person consistently made decisions to spend his new earnings wisely so that he would again reach millionaire status.

His self-image motivated him to work hard, save his money, and to invest wisely so that he would again become a millionaire, where he was comfortable.

Oh no! But I was only trying to help!

Have you ever had this experience?

Let's say that you sponsored someone with poor finances. You wanted to help him succeed.

You worked hard. You picked him up for training. You made his phone calls for him. You bought products for him. You even sponsored a few distributors and placed them in his organization! In other words, you did everything you knew to help him get ahead in your business.

And after all that work, he failed. Nothing happened.

* He never developed an organization.

* He never called the distributors you sponsored for him.

* His relatives came to visit him on the night of the important meeting.

* He had to work overtime instead of picking up that hot prospect.

* He forgot about ordering products last month.

* He invested his overtime check in lottery tickets instead of sponsoring tools.

* He said that he was afraid to call his friends.

* He didn't feel right about approaching his relatives.

* He said that he wasn't good at talking to strangers.

* He didn't have time to go to training.

* He talked to the distributors you placed under him, and actually got them to quit the business!

See the picture?

He is doing everything possible to fail, to stay right where he is financially, because he is comfortable with his self-image as someone who is struggling financially.

No matter how much you try to help this person, he will sabotage your efforts.

If he earns a bonus check, he will spend it on personal items instead of building his business.

If his downline starts to grow, he will remind them of all the problems that will keep them from succeeding.

Nothing you can do will make this person successful.

The only way this person can become successful is to **change** his self-image. And that is an inside job. That is something he has to do.

And changing your self-image is very, very uncomfortable.

Why?

Because you first have to admit what your present self-image is.

What is your self-image right now?

Here is a quick way to get a pretty good idea of your self-image. Ready?

Think of exactly where you are right now.

That's it.

That is your self-image.

For example, what is your financial self-image? (Yes, there is more to life than finances, but we are only going to talk about this one self-image now.)

* If you're making $1,000 a month, then you have a $1,000 self-image.

* If you're making $5,000 a month, then you have a $5,000 self-image.

* If you're making $10,000 a month, then you have a $10,000 a month self-image.

Simple, isn't it?

The **hard** part is to **admit** that this is our self-image. Most of us hate to take personal responsibility for our circumstances.

Now there will be a few exceptions.

For instance, if we visit the social welfare recipient the day after he wins the lottery, well, he is rich that day. But he is actively working to get back to his self-image.

Or, if we visit the former millionaire the day after he goes bankrupt, well, he is broke that day. But that is not his self-image. He is actively working to get back to his millionaire status and lifestyle.

How do you know if someone is in transition like the social welfare lottery winner or the former millionaire?

When that person is actively working to **change** his present circumstances. When that person is highly motivated to overcome any obstacle or problem in his way.

You see, true motivation only comes when our outside circumstances **don't match** our self-image.

But for most of us, we are actively **living** our self-image.

Are you happy with your present financial self-image?

It's easy to tell.

If you are working hard ...

overcoming obstacles, objections and problems, that would mean that your present financial circumstances are **less** than your current financial self-image. You are highly motivated to improve your outside circumstances to match your self-image.

If you are content where you are ...

occasionally attending meetings, occasionally making a presentation or two, then your present outside circumstances **match** your current financial self-image. Of course you might say otherwise, but your actions speak louder than words. You will continue to avoid rejection, making new and harder commitments, and you'll simply enjoy life as it is.

If you are sabotaging your business ...

complaining about the compensation plan, worrying about the cost of the products, passing on your depressing thoughts to your upline and downline, campaigning for a change in the company newsletter, worrying about corporate and distributor politics, then your present outside circumstances are **greater** than your current self-image. You will continue to sabotage your business until you lower your income to match your current self-image. Then you will feel comfortable.

And your outside circumstances won't change until you change your self-image.

For example, my current weight is 170 pounds. I'm comfortable with that weight. I am not motivated to lose weight even though I'm 20 pounds overweight.

Sure, I talk about losing weight, I set goals to lose weight, I exercise on occasion, but no matter what I do, I seem to eat just enough and to exercise just enough to remain at 170 pounds.

So, what do you think my self-image is about my weight?

I see myself as 170 pounds.

And nothing will change until I change my self-image of 170 pounds. Diets won't work, exercise won't work, health spas won't work, different food choices won't work, and well, you get the picture.

Don't listen and don't believe me when I say I want to lose weight.

Instead, simply observe where I am today. That's my self-image.

(On a side note, I am thinking about changing my self-image about my weight. I'm considering a new self-image of 180 pounds so that I can eat more Mexican food.)

Don't listen to your distributors!

Instead, simply **observe** where they are today. Watch for signs of motivation to improve, or motivation to sabotage their business. Their actions will speak so loudly you won't have to listen to how much they "want it" or what "big goals" they are setting.

These words are meaningless. They just help your distributor feel like they are doing something while remaining within the safety of their current self-image.

Take this test.

Q. A new distributor approaches you and says:

"I just don't have any prospects. I don't have anybody to talk to. Could you run an ad for me? Could you find me some people to talk to?"

Your response is:

1. Run an ad. Even though your distributor doesn't have enough motivation to find someone to talk to, you feel that a $200 ad will make him successful.

2. Every morning you go door-to-door, approaching strangers. If a stranger is willing to listen, you say: "Wait. Let me get my new distributor so he can talk to you."

3. Give your new distributor a 30-minute audio on how to find more prospects. Even though your distributor has already listened to 121 audio trainings, you feel your new distributor is just one audio training message away from success.

4. Say to your new distributor, "Let's talk about self-image. Let's talk about how we decide to become successful or unsuccessful. Let's learn how our minds really work."

So, which option did you choose? I hope you chose option #4.

Okay, next question in this test.

Q. A new distributor approaches you and says:

"The products don't work, the company is in the wrong city, the newsletter is wrinkled, the compensation plan isn't fair, the competition is perfect, and my dog bit me."

Your response is:

1. Find new products, help the home office move to another city, use a hot iron on his newsletter, give him more than his fair share from the compensation plan, give the competition some problems, and buy a muzzle for his dog.

2. Personally quit your business in despair.

3. Take up drinking.

4. Say to your new distributor, "Let's talk about self-image. Let's talk about how we decide to become successful or unsuccessful. Let's learn how our minds really work."

So, which option did you choose? Again, I hope you chose option #4.

But how do I increase a potential leader's self-image?

The short explanation:

"Personal development."

Self-image and confidence comes from within. For decades, network marketing leaders have guided people to motivational books, positive attitude seminars, and personal development CDs.

Ask yourself, "Are my potential leaders studying personal development books or audios? What are they doing to improve their self-image and confidence?"

If the answer is, "Nothing," then the entire task lies with you. And do you think you have enough time in the day to constantly praise the potential leader? To compliment him on every step forward? To read positive affirmations to him before he goes to sleep?

Probably not.

Developing this self-image and confidence is something that your potential leader can do on his own, while you are investing your time teaching him the skills of leadership.

Make it easy on yourself. Get your potential leaders into a habit of books and audios.

Developing one's self-image and confidence can be done while mastering how one thinks about problems. This first step towards leadership is a big step, so start now.

Free!

Get 7 mini-reports of amazing, easy sentences that create new, hot prospects.

Discover how just a **few correct words** can change your network marketing results forever.

Get all seven <u>free</u> Big Al mini-reports, and the <u>free</u> weekly Big Al Report with more recruiting and prospecting tips.

Sign up today at:
http://www.BigAlReport.com

Want Big Al to speak in your area?

Request a Big Al training event:
http://www.BigAlSeminars.com

Tom "Big Al" Schreiter's books
are available at:
http://www.BigAlBooks.com

See a full line of Big Al products at:
http://www.FortuneNow.com

ABOUT THE AUTHOR

Tom "Big Al" Schreiter has 40+ years of experience in network marketing and MLM. As the author of the original "Big Al" training books in the late '70s, he has continued to speak in over 80 countries on using the exact words and phrases to get prospects to open up their minds and say "YES."

His passion is marketing ideas, marketing campaigns, and how to speak to the subconscious mind in simplified, practical ways. He is always looking for case studies of incredible marketing campaigns that give usable lessons.

As the author of numerous audio trainings, Tom is a favorite speaker at company conventions and regional events.

Visit Tom's blog for a regular update of network marketing and MLM business-building ideas.

http://www.BigAlBlog.com

Anyone can subscribe to his free weekly tips at:

http://www.BigAlReport.com

60896728R00082

Made in the USA
Lexington, KY
22 February 2017